# 40 DAYS
# OF PRAYER

Connecting Your Needs
to the Power of God!

Pastor Will Stoll

Northwest Church
Fresno, California
www.nwc.org

All scriptures are quoted in the New International Version unless otherwise noted.
THE HOLY BIBLE, NEW INTERNATIONAL VERSION®, NIV® Copyright © 1973, 1978, 198
2011 by Biblica, Inc.™ Used by permission. All rights reserved worldwide.

ISBN: 978-0-9915559-1-8
Published by Perfect Marketing Team, Fresno, CA
Design and layout by Nancy Avera
Printed in the United States of America

# CONTENTS

Foreword _____ iii

Acknowledgements _____ iv

Introduction _____ 1

## WEEK 1 | WHY PRAY?

DAY 1    Why Pray? Our Needs Are Huge! _____ 5

DAY 2    Why Pray? God Loves to Answer Prayer _____ 9

DAY 3    Why Pray? Our Nation Needs It _____ 13

DAY 4    Why Pray? It is a Necessary & Solitary Release _____ 17

DAY 5    Why Pray? God Beats Our Expectations _____ 21

DAY 6    Why Pray? We Get God's Peace _____ 25

DAY 7    Why Pray? The End is Near _____ 29

## WEEK 2 | GETTING RESULTS

DAY 8    Getting Results - Praying in Faith _____ 35

DAY 9    Getting Results - Asking! _____ 39

DAY 10   Getting Results - Giving God Your All _____ 43

DAY 11   Getting Results - Giving God Your ALL _____ 47

DAY 12   Getting Results - Praying in God's Will _____ 51

DAY 13   Getting Results - Dealing with Different Results _____ 55

DAY 14   Getting Results - Praying in Jesus' Name _____ 59

## WEEK 3 | MEETING GOD

DAY 15   Meeting God - Your First Meeting _____ 65

DAY 16   Meeting God - Walking with God _____ 69

DAY 17   Meeting God - Expect Your Faith to Grow _____ 73

DAY 18   Meeting God - Your Light Intensifies _____ 77

DAY 19   Meeting God - Your Perspective Changes _____ 81

DAY 20   Meeting God - Your Concerns Change _____ 85

DAY 21   Meeting God - Get to Know Him By Name _____ 89

## WEEK 4 | THE SCHOOL OF PRAYER

DAY 22   The School of Prayer – Professor Paul _____ 95

DAY 23   The School of Prayer – Professor Jesus The Lord's Prayer _____ 101

DAY 24    THE SCHOOL OF PRAYER – PROFESSOR JESUS THE LORD'S PRAYER_____ 107

DAY 25    THE SCHOOL OF PRAYER – PROFESSOR JABEZ _____ 113

DAY 26    THE SCHOOL OF PRAYER – PROFESSOR JACOB _____ 117

DAY 27    THE SCHOOL OF PRAYER – PRAYING WITH OTHERS _____ 121

DAY 28    THE SCHOOL OF PRAYER – PRACTICING PRAYER _____ 125

## WEEK 5 | PRAYER EXTINGUISHERS

DAY 29    PRAYER EXTINGUISHERS – UNCONFESSED SIN _____ 131

DAY 30    PRAYER EXTINGUISHERS – PRIDE _____ 135

DAY 31    PRAYER EXTINGUISHERS – DIVISION_____ 141

DAY 32    PRAYER EXTINGUISHERS – SAYING "NO"_____ 145

DAY 33    PRAYER EXTINGUISHERS – FAILURE TO FORGIVE _____ 149

DAY 34    PRAYER EXTINGUISHERS – IDOLATRY _____ 153

DAY 35    PRAYER EXTINGUISHERS – GRUMBLING _____ 157

## WEEK 6 | TIME & PRAYER

DAY 36    TIME & PRAYER – TAKING TIME TO PRAY _____ 163

DAY 37    TIME & PRAYER – THE HOUR OF PRAYER _____ 169

DAY 38    TIME & PRAYER – PRAYING WITHOUT CEASING _____ 175

DAY 39    TIME & PRAYER – MAKING A PRAYER LIST _____ 179

DAY 40    TIME & PRAYER – LEAVING A LEGACY_____ 183

# FOREWORD

In the midst of so many books on prayer, Pastor Will Stoll's book, *40 Days of Prayer* is a refreshing attempt to mobilize the church to pray. Will has modeled a life saturated with prayer. His transparency through life's challenges and his deep dependence on prayer provides the basis for this 40-day guide for anyone to follow.

Pastor Will does not approach this book as a theologian or a spiritual guru, but writes from a heart of humility, as one who has been rewarded by much grace through prayer. The *40 Days of Prayer* are organized in a logical and stimulating way to lead the average person into a deeper level of prayer. Pastor Will addresses many of the major issues of prayer and invites us to enter the school of prayer with the great men and women of the Bible. He masterfully guides the reader in dealing with obstacles that sabotage our efforts toward a consistent prayer life.

I am personally excited about joining Will on this journey of prayer. If someone is willing to make the commitment to follow this excellent guide to *40 Days of Prayer*, I believe that it will bring them into a deeper relationship with Jesus Christ.

– Dr. Jim Westgate

# ACKNOWLEDGEMENTS

First and foremost I want to thank God, He is my source of strength and deserves all the glory. This book began as a series of off-the-cuff video devotionals that I recorded back in 2007. I was doing a message series on prayer and thought that it would be nice to encourage our congregation to dig deeper during the week. I had always hoped that those devotional thoughts would find a larger audience than just You-Tube. Five years later, those thoughts became a book. It took an amazing team of individuals to transform those videos into what you are holding. I need to thank Carol Tickvitza, my assistant, who transcribed each video. I would also like to thank Matt Shores and Jeremy Dager who provided research assistance.

There was another team of individuals who joyfully read my chicken scratch before asking, "What were you trying to say again?" Thank you Darrell Fifield, Greg Sumii, Jeff Rickels and Sid Cox. Your contributions spared readers from witnessing what I did to the King's English. (I ain't even kidding!) Thanks, guys.

Nancy Avera prayed for hours as she worked on a book about prayer. She tirelessly designed and laid out each page of the book, its cover and contents. Thank you for all of the extra hours you put into making this book look great.

And finally, I want to thank Katie, my wife, for the years of prayer and support she has given to me. Without Katie's encouragement this book would not be possible.

– Pastor Will Stoll

# INTRODUCTION

Does the world really need another book about prayer? That's the question I was asking myself one night on a walk with my eight-month-old baby, Abbey, strapped to me in a front pack. I remember praying, "Who am I to write this book? I'm not good at praying. I'm not faithful like those people who pray for hours and never run out of things to say."

Just before our walk ended, I looked down at the back of Abagail's head – it was perfect; I remember praying, "Lord, let this little girl find You as Savior at the earliest possible age. Then allow her to serve You the rest of her life and bring people to You."

That would have been a great place for me to stop. Any father would be proud of those blessings to come upon one of his children. But for some reason, really as an afterthought, I continued, "and Lord, even as a baby, let her bring people to know You." I'll never know why I prayed for that. It didn't even make sense at the time. Babies do not preach sermons or tell people about Jesus. But I wasn't too worried about the logic of the prayer. I just prayed what I felt in my heart. Little did I know that the next day Abagail would change our lives forever.

## MY GAME CHANGING MOMENT

The next day began as a typical Friday for us. My wife, Katie, and I dropped our three older girls off at school. We spent the morning together with Abbey (our weekly "date" together). This particular Friday was different because our church was hosting a family camp in the mountains that would begin later that evening. This meant my late afternoon would include a trip to the R.V. rental store to get a pop-up trailer.

As the day pressed on toward 2:30 p.m., I was hurrying to borrow a friend's truck that had the necessary air brakes to handle a trailer. Right before leaving the house, I said goodbye to Katie, then I offered to take Abbey with me so Katie could pick up the kids from school and finish packing. So I scooped little Abbey up, put her in the car seat and away we went.

My friend's house is only a mile away from our home with no stop-lights in between. On the way over, I received several phone calls. The first from the rental company telling me the pop-up trailer I reserved had not been returned. They continued with more bad news, that my insurance company had not completed the necessary paperwork and I needed to contact them. In the middle of this call, my friend phoned to say he was running thirty minutes late.

This was a lot to process in a one-mile drive. By now Abbey was fast asleep. We waited in my friend's driveway while I called insurance agents and rental companies. When my friend arrived I helped him un-load his trailer and we quickly hopped in his car and headed for the R.V. store 30 minutes away.

After we arrived at the R.V. store, there were a few more problems and delays. But at long last, I rented a full-blown motor home. I was about to get behind the wheel of this rig when my wife called. I explained how I needed to rent something a bit bigger and I wouldn't be much longer. She kindly sympathized with me and asked, "How is Abbey doing?" The ink you see on this paper will never convey the overwhelming feeling of despair that instantly swallowed me in that moment. I had forgotten Abbey. I left her in my car at my friend's house. I screamed, "Oh God, I left her in the car!" I cried out desperately, "God help her!" I certainly couldn't. I was a helpless 30 minutes away. Abbey had been in that car for over an hour in nearly 100 degree heat.

## THE MIRACLE

*"The angel of the LORD encamps around those who fear him, and he delivers them." Psalm 34:7*

After a call to the home where the car was parked, my friend's wife opened the car door, and Abbey smiled and reached out to hug her. Moments later my wife arrived. Together they cooled Abbey off in the kitchen sink while she played in the water.

Minutes later the paramedics arrived at the door. My wife carried Abbey out to them. Perplexed, they asked, "Where is the baby that was left in the car?" Abbey had no signs of heat stroke. The fire chief of 22 years told my wife, "This never happens." He continued, "On a day like this, a baby left in a vehicle often dies in less than thirty minutes."

As a precaution, we took Abbey to the hospital and thankfully she was released in less than one hour with no signs of any harm. She did not have a fever, her oxygen levels were 100 percent normal and my wife and I were in disbelief. Again and again we wondered aloud, "Is she really okay?" Initially, our human minds would not accept God's work at face value. I knew Abagail was unharmed. Was this His miracle? The next day, God allowed that question to be answered.

For the first time, Abbey spoke. She said, "Mama." Everything before that morning was typical baby cooing. She had never uttered a real discernible word until that point in her life. And to show off a little more – as if talking was not evidence enough – she stood up. Abbey had only started to crawl a few weeks before. But while sitting next to our bed she grabbed the wrought iron post and stood up for the first time.

## WHY WRITE THIS STUFF?

Why would I tell you this story? Because I'm a man full of flaws, bumps and bruises. During those tense moments on that hot afternoon, I experienced emotions that I can't describe and really don't want to revisit. I thought my precious baby was dead, and it was my fault. But that's not how this story ended.

The story continues to reveal that God's power outshines my weakness. Truly, I was powerless, but the strength of Jesus sustained my family and me. Without knowing it, I wrote this book for anyone who feels powerless to change what has happened or is happening in their lives. If you feel overwhelmed by emotions of despair, emptiness, and inadequacy; if you are helplessly at the end of your rope, this book will be helpful to you.

The truth is that all of us will have difficult times. We don't know when, but they definitely will come. How do you prepare for these times ahead? Learn to pray.

## WHAT WILL THIS BOOK DELIVER?

This book will teach you how to connect to God. That is all. I can't say that this book will serve as an instruction manual to get everything you want from God. He may not perform a miracle for you like I witnessed. But when you learn to connect to God, you connect to His great love, His unlimited power, and His promises that will give you hope.

# DAY 1

*Why Pray? Our Needs Are Huge!*

*"God will meet all your needs according to the riches of his glory in Christ Jesus."*
Philippians 4:19

*"God does nothing but by prayer, and everything with it."*
John Wesley – 1800s Theologian

Imagine getting into your car to go to work. When you turn the key, nothing happens. After a few simple checks you realize you have no clue what's wrong. So you call a mechanic. Why? Because you have a need and the mechanic can meet it. We pray for the same reason. We have big issues, bigger than a broken down car, and God is the only one who can meet those needs.

## PHYSICAL NEEDS

So the first reason we need to pray is that our needs are huge. Most of our needs fall into four categories: physical, spiritual, emotional, and intellectual. First, there are physical needs. The Bible puts it this way, "And the prayer offered in faith will make the sick person well..." (James 5:15) While God does not physically heal everyone who asks (if

He did, Adam and Eve would probably still be running around) there are hundreds of biblical examples where He does heal. God wants us to bring our health needs to Him.

However, God cares about more than just our health. A recent survey showed that 78% of prayers are related to health and safety.[1] If you have ever attended a church prayer meeting you know that is true. One Christian counselor wrote, "Many pastoral prayers sound uncannily like a nursing report at shift change in your local hospital."[2] Health concerns, while important, are not our only physical needs.

We need food, shelter and clothing. That's why Jesus said, "Pray like this...give us this day our daily bread." (Matthew 6:11) One passage of scripture says, "Give me neither poverty nor riches, but give me only my daily bread." (Proverbs 30:8) Praying for all daily physical needs acknowledges that God is the provider and sustainer in all areas of our life and admits your need for Him in everything.

## SPIRITUAL NEEDS

We all have spiritual needs. Until we enter into a relationship with God we have a huge void in our lives. The Bible teaches that we are born spiritually dead – that is, we lack a relationship with God. The Apostle Paul says, "As for you, you were dead in your transgressions and sins." (Ephesians 2:1) The greatest spiritual need we have is to be forgiven of our sins and made alive. We will talk more about this on day 15.

After you meet God, there is still a need for daily cleansing. If you've ever met a Christian you know that we are not perfect to say the least. This is why Jesus teaches us to pray, "Forgive us our debts as we also have forgiven our debtors." (Matthew 6:12) This need for forgiveness is met when we confess our faults to God. At this point we begin a lifelong

---

1   http://www.beliefnet.com/Faiths/Faith-Tools/Meditation/2004/12/U-S-News-Beliefnet-Prayer-Survey-Results.aspx

2   David Powlison, "Prayer Beyond the Sick List," The Journal of Biblical Counseling (Winter, 2005); 2.

process of growing in our faith. This forgiveness brings God's peace to our hearts so that we can forgive others.

## EMOTIONAL NEEDS

We also have emotional needs. We need intimacy; to know someone and to be known. The Bible says, "There is a friend who sticks closer than a brother." (Proverbs 18:24) The writer is talking about Jesus. You get close to people by trusting them with your personal information – the real you. We get close to God in the same way.

We all need love. Spending time with God and seeing His involvement in our circumstances assures us of His love for us. Also, when we pray in Jesus' Name, it reminds us of the cross. It was on the cross that Jesus died as our substitute. He took on Himself the penalty for our sins. After suffering a cruel death on the cross He arose from the grave on the third day, conquering sin and death. There is no way to look at the cross and not realize that God loves us dearly.

We need to feel hope and acceptance. As you spend time with your Creator, you realize that He created you for a reason. "For I know the plans I have for you," declares the Lord, "plans to prosper you and not to harm you, plans to give you hope and a future." (Jeremiah 29:11) As you pray, God begins to reveal His plan for your life. His plan will probably not come as a lightning bolt, or handwriting on the wall. He usually works day-by-day, revealing His plan for you little by little. It is a better plan that any human mind could conceive.

## INTELLECTUAL NEEDS

Lastly, we have intellectual needs. We have a longing to understand our world and our experiences. That is what philosophy attempts to accomplish. Your worldview is dramatically altered by spending time in God's Word and in His presence. Solomon had just been given the keys to the greatest kingdom on earth. His father David had died; now he was the man! Shortly after taking the throne, God offered Solomon one wish. This was Solomon's response, "So give your servant a discerning heart to govern your people and to distinguish between right and wrong." (1 Kings 3:9) God was so impressed with Solomon's request for understanding that He made him the wisest and richest man alive! We can ask God for wisdom. "If any of you lacks wisdom, he should ask God, who gives generously to all without finding fault, and it will be given to him." (James 1:5) The need for wisdom might be your greatest need. Whether you are facing relational problems, an illness, a job loss, or nursing a broken heart – you need God's wisdom during this time in your life.

Our needs are huge! Nobody understood this like George Mueller. He was the founder of five orphanages during the 19th century. He decided early on to never solicit donations, but instead to trust that God would provide for their needs. On one occasion the orphanages ran out of food. When the children woke up, Mueller called everyone to the breakfast and prayed for food to be provided. Moments later a bread truck stalled outside their door. The driver politely asked if the orphanage could use some bread that would otherwise have to be thrown away. Please remember that God does not always answer this quickly or in the way that we think He should. However, this is one of thousands of answered prayers in Mueller's life. He would later write:

> "Everyone is invited and commanded to trust in the Lord, to trust in Him with all your heart, and to cast his burden upon Him, and to call upon Him in the day of trouble. Will you not do this?"[3]

We need to pray. So today I challenge you, spend time with God.

---

3   http://www.desiringgod.org/resource-library/biographies/george-muellers-strategy-for-showing-god#84

# DAY 2

*Why Pray? God Loves to Answer Prayer*

*"Then you will call,
and the LORD will answer."*
Isaiah 58:9

*"Four things let us ever keep in mind: God
hears prayer, God heeds prayer, God answers
prayer, and God delivers by prayer."*
E.M. Bounds – Minister 1800s

I have four incredible daughters. I love to give them the things they like. Reilly, 6 years old, loves stuffed animals. So I look for special occasions when I can bring home a stuffed bunny or a horse all wrapped up. I get joy seeing her face light up as she opens that gift. However, she also loves fireworks, which I recognize might be dangerous for her and the neighborhood. So I don't give her fireworks, but I still love her. Although she doesn't know it, giving her fireworks is not in anyone's best interest. Since I know that, I keep them far from her.

God operates in much the same way. God is omniscient, He knows everything, including my needs and what is best for me. He delights in answering our prayers, and meeting our needs! Jesus says, "Ask and it will be given to you; seek and you will find; knock and the door will be opened to you." (Matthew 7:7) God loves to give us things as an answer, but He prefers to be the answer. The Bible says, "Then you will call, and the Lord will answer; you will cry for help, and he will say: 'Here am I.'" (Isaiah 58:9) God says, "Relax, I'm here. I am the answer to your prayer!"

## WHY ASK?

Maybe you are wondering why God tells us to ask when He already knows our need. A.A. Hodge, a popular biblical commentator, provides a helpful analogy. He says,

> "Does God know the day you'll die? Yes. Has he appointed that day? Yes. Can you do anything to change that day? No. Then why do you eat? To live. What happens if you don't eat? You die. Then if you don't eat, and die, then would that be the day that God had appointed for you to die?…Quit asking stupid questions and just eat. Eating is the pre-ordained way God has appointed for living."

Prayer is the way we get in line with God's way of accomplishing His purposes. The Bible is full of stories that illustrate this truth.

## WINNING BATTLES

Take for example Exodus 17, where the Israelites are in battle. When Moses raises his hands in prayer the Israelites start winning – when he lowers his hands they start losing. In Joshua 10, the Israelites are in a battle and Joshua prays for the sun to stand still, and it did! Prayer changes things because God answers prayer.

## FAMILY PLANNING

In Genesis 24, Abraham sent his servant to find a wife for his son, Isaac. His servant stops at a well and prays, "Lord, let the person he is supposed to marry come to this well and let her offer to water my camels when I ask her for a drink for myself." The Bible says in Genesis 24,

"Before he had finished praying, Rebekah came walking up with her water and offered to water all of his camels." That's a fast answer by any standard.

After Rebekah and Isaac were married, they discovered that she was unable to bear children. So when Isaac prayed for children, you guessed it, Rebekah became pregnant. God answers prayer.

## "PLAGUE FREE" LIVING

At one point during Israel's history, the Egyptians enslaved them. God sent Moses to Pharaoh (Egypt's ruler) with this message, "Let my people go!" When Pharaoh refused to let his enslaved workforce go, God sent 10 plagues throughout the whole land of Egypt. After the second plague (frogs), Pharaoh relented, and agreed to let Israel go. So Moses asked that God remove the frogs. The Bible says, "And the Lord did what Moses asked. The frogs died in the houses, in the courtyards and in the fields." (Exodus 8:13) Later Pharaoh changed his mind; he wondered how his massive public works projects would be accomplished without the slaves. So God sent locusts to cause Pharaoh to let them go. The locusts caused Pharaoh's mind to change back – okay they can go free! Moses prayed that the locusts would go away. The Bible says, "And the Lord changed the wind to a very strong west wind, which caught up the locusts and carried them into the Red Sea. Not a locust was left anywhere in Egypt." (Exodus 10:19)

## NATIONAL ISSUES

Daniel was part of a nation that was running from God, so he prayed a national prayer of repentance. While he was still praying, Gabriel came and said, "As soon as you began to pray, an answer was given, which I have come to tell you, for you are highly esteemed." (Daniel 9:23) Gabriel gave Daniel a vision, which was his answer to prayer.

Jonah was part of a national crisis. Nineveh needed the news about a

God who loved and created them. Since he was unwilling to give them the message, God sent a storm to get Jonah's attention. Then He sent a fish to swallow him to protect his messenger. After three days in the fish's stomach, Jonah prayed, "Lord, I'd like the opportunity to preach in Nineveh." The Bible says, "And the Lord commanded the fish, and it vomited Jonah onto dry land."(Jonah 2:10) God answered his prayer while at the same time providing a message of hope for the city of Nineveh.

## HELP FOR LIVING

After Jesus' ascension into heaven, the disciples got together in a room and prayed something like this, "Help Lord, we need You." The Bible says, "After they prayed, the place where they were meeting was shaken. And they were all filled with the Holy Spirit and spoke the word of God boldly."(Acts 4:31) You can go through every page of your Bible and find people who prayed just like that. These people got the help they needed from God. I would encourage you to read your Bible with a colored marker in hand so you can highlight all the answers to prayer you find. If you do that, you will find that God loves to answer prayer.

Do you need some help? Ask the Lord God Almighty for His help. So today read through some of these amazing true stories in Scripture. Take joy in the fact that God does answer prayer. What are you waiting for? Go pray!

# DAY 3

*Why Pray? Our Nation Needs It*

*"I urge, then, first of all, that petitions, prayers,*
*intercession and thanksgiving be made for all*
*people – for kings and all those in authority..."*
1 *Timothy 2:1-2*

*"To get nations back on their feet,*
*we must first get down on our knees."*
*Billy Graham – Evangelist*

America is in trouble. We have 15 trillion dollars of national debt that we add to daily. As I write this we have a Congress with a record low approval rating of 10%. We are hitting hard times, but not for the reasons that one might think. The root of our problem is morality. America has a lust addiction. There are more than 24 million pornographic websites. Forty million Americans are regular visitors to porn sites. In the United States, porn pulls in $2.84 billion dollars a year. The average age at which a child views porn is 11 years![1]

I don't have to tell you that adultery is commonplace. "It is conservatively estimated that 30% of all married individuals (in the United States) will engage in infidelity at some point during their marriage."[2]

---

1  http://gizmodo.com/5552899/finally-some-actual-stats-on-internet-porn

2  It is no surprise that 50% of marriages end in divorce. However, what might surprise you is that there is only a .00086% divorce rate among couple that pray together each day. That is 1 divorce in 1152 marriages. Prayer is the best marriage insurance I know about. (http://marriageoutreach.com/praying-together)

We are teaching our young students that homosexuality and gay marriage are normative behavior.[3] These facts could easily lead one to lose hope. However, Charles Spurgeon, a 19th Century pastor and author, in his book titled *Finding Peace in Life's Storms,* reminds us, "Jesus lives and is as able to deal with these cases of distress and sorrow as when He was here below…No situation will ever be hard for Him. We only have to bring our needs to Him."

Who is to blame for the moral condition in which we find ourselves? Jesus said that believers are to be the salt that preserves the world from decay. This is why God makes the activity of believers the pre-requisite for revival.[4] In scripture God says,

> "If my people, who are called by my name, will humble themselves and pray and seek my face and turn from their wicked ways, then will I hear from heaven and will forgive their sin and will heal their land." (2 Chronicles 7:14)

According to this verse, believers must engage in three activities before our land will be healed.

## HUMBLE OURSELVES

First, we need to "humble ourselves and pray." Who could forget 9/11? Almost everyone in America was praying. That lasted about two weeks, and then we forgot that we needed God, and went back to our usual lives. We have to get on our knees and humble ourselves and tell God that we know that we need Him.

---

3  In fact even as I write this New York State has just passed a same sex marriage law making it the largest state to allow same sex marriages (http://www.nytimes.com/2011/06/25/nyregion/gay-marriage-approved-by-new-york-senate.html?pagewanted=all)

4  Revival is a special occurrence in history when God reaches down from heaven and awakens His people in a unique and transformational way. The result of revival is inevitably that God's people begin to love and share Jesus with people they know.

# DESPERATELY SEEK GOD

Second, we have to desperately seek God's face. Uganda has seen massive spiritual and sociological changes over the last three decades. When you walk down the street, you see businesses with names like, "The Holy Spirit Hair Salon" and "The Trinity Ice Cream Parlor." Many social and political leaders are believers. What a change from 34 years ago. The government was thoroughly corrupt. Idi Amin was murdering his own citizens en masse daily. Their only hope was for God to save them. When believers prayed desperately (usually huddled together in clandestine jungle prayer meetings) God responded powerfully. Today they have an entirely different government. First Lady Museveni prays publicly and openly encourages people to trust in Jesus. Twice daily nationally sponsored public radio hosts intercessory prayer.

This shouldn't surprise us – throughout scripture, desperate prayer preceded times of revival. David Platt, a contemporary pastor and author, notes, "Every major breakthrough for the church in the book of Acts came about as a direct result of prayer. God performed mighty works for the propagation of the Gospel and the declaration of His glory in direct proportion of the prayers of His people."[5]

America needs revival, but we will not see it until we are desperate for God. Let's not wait for a nationally devastating event to get serious about seeking God.

# REPENT

Third, we need to turn from our wicked ways. It is the sin of believers that offends God. He doesn't expect unbelievers to be morally upright. The problem is that pornography, adultery and every imaginable offense has crept into the lives of believers. We must repent if God is going to heal our country.

---

5   David Platt, *Radical Together*, 83.

Once Pastor Joe Wright was asked to pray for our country in the Kansas House of Representatives. He prayed:

> "Heavenly Father, we come before You today to ask Your forgiveness and to seek Your direction and guidance. We know Your Word says 'woe to those who call evil good' but that's exactly what we've done. We have lost our spiritual equilibrium and reversed our values. We have exploited the poor and called it lottery. We have rewarded laziness and called it welfare. We have killed our unborn and called it choice. We have shot abortionists and called it justifiable. We have coveted our neighbors' possessions and called it ambition. We have polluted the air with pornography and profanity and called it freedom of expression. We have ridiculed the time-honored values of our forefathers and called it enlightenment. Search us, oh God, and know our hearts today. Cleanse us from every sin and set us free. Amen"

God bless you as you pray for our nation in great need. Pray also for your own humility and repentance.

# DAY 4

*Why Pray? It is a Necessary*
*& Solitary Release*

"*I cry aloud to the LORD; I lift up my voice to*
*the LORD for mercy. I pour out before him*
*my complaint; before him I tell my trouble.*"
Psalm 142

"*He who has learned to pray has learned the*
*greatest secret of a holy and happy life.*"
William Law – Spiritual Writer 1700s

## THE HOLY RELEASE VALVE

Expressing your emotions is a critical part of life. When it happens in the right way it acts like a pressure relief valve that can help both physically and emotionally. In other words, it can keep you from saying things you regret or doing things that are inappropriate. On the other hand, it can be very harmful if you hold things inside. The University of Texas conducted a study on the side effects of "bottled-up" emotion. The study suggests that people who do not express their emotions are more likely to act out aggressively. Other studies have shown that pent up feelings cause irritability, anxiety, depression, heart disease, etc. Does this sound familiar?

Prayer is the only way that we can express our innermost feelings and emotions to God. Whether we are communicating to God through songs, in written or spoken words, it all boils down to prayer. Sure, God knows about my needs, problems, and desires before I do, but it is still therapeutic – not to mention commanded – that I express these things to Him.

## DAVID - A GREAT MODEL OF PRAYER RELEASE

David's life included a constant barrage of stressful events. As a shepherd he was required to protect his sheep. Sometimes this meant fighting a bear or a lion at a moment's notice. As a harpist for King Saul he would have dodged a spear on more than one occasion. As King he fought battles, broke up conspiracies and thwarted assassination plots hatched by his own son. He would bury several of his children under disparaging circumstances. How did he keep things together during trying times? David activated the release valve of prayer.

David is a role model for us. He was not afraid to say to God what most of us only think. Like, "How long, O Lord? Will you forget me forever? How long will you hide your face from me?" (Psalm 13:1) That's not the kind of thing you hear in the prayer before church or an evening meal. Yet so often we feel forgotten and alone. We should express those feelings to God.

Other times David felt great resolve to trust God. He declares, "The Lord is my rock, my fortress and my deliverer; my God is my rock, in whom I take refuge, my shield and the horn of my salvation, my stronghold." (Psalm 18:2) When God directly answers a prayer of yours, or you see Him do something wonderful and unexpected, you feel like that, too. Express that to God.

After David had committed the sin of adultery with Bathsheba, he compounded the felony by murdering her husband, Uriah. When confronted about his sins by Nathan (a prophet of God), David responds with a great prayer of repentance unlike anything the world has seen documented before. It is a prayer that is repeated again and again every day all over the world. He said, "Have mercy on me O God; according to your abundant mercy, blot out my transgressions." (Psalm 51:1) I would encourage you to take a moment to read all of Psalm 51. It is a great chapter.

Still other times David released his emotions by praising God. He writes, "O Lord, our Lord, how majestic is your name in all the earth!" (Psalm 8:1) In this Psalm, David declares that he is overwhelmed as he looks at the stars that God made and again at the delicate life of a newborn child. He is overwhelmed by God's plan that man would rule the animals and the earth itself. "What a plan," David says.

## DIVINE ATTENTION

What caused David to pray so patiently and fervently? Faith. He believed that God was listening attentively to what he was saying. However, when you use the same technique with men, you can be easily disillusioned. Maybe you've had the experience of pouring your heart out to a friend or even a paid counselor, and at some point in the conversation it becomes clear that they are "somewhere else." They are present physically, but mentally checked out. Most of us react to that by withdrawing from the conversation and sometimes even the relationship. It's pointless to expose your feelings to someone who is not willing to listen in earnest. God is nothing like a disinterested friend or counselor. David's prayers rose out of that conviction. He wrote, "You know when I sit down and when I rise up; You discern my thoughts from afar. You search out my path and my lying down and are acquainted with all my ways. Even before a word is on my tongue, behold, O Lord, You know it altogether." (Psalm 139:2-4) David goes on to say that there is no way to get away from God even if we wanted to.

Since God is ever present, ever caring, and ever able to act upon what we tell Him, why not tell Him first and tell Him everything? Open up the release valve of your thoughts, feelings, and emotions. Tell God what's really going on in your life.

# DAY 5

*Why Pray? God Beats Our Expectations*

*"Now to Him who is able to do immeasurably
more than all we ask or imagine..."*
*Ephesians 3:20*

*"Beware in your prayers, above everything else, of
limiting God, not only by unbelief, but by fancy-
ing that you know what He can do. Expect unexpected things 'above all that we ask or think'."*
*Andrew Murray – Writer & Teacher*

Have you ever received a gift that was far greater than you were expecting? I remember on my fifth birthday I asked for a Lego castle. I really wanted a train set that I had seen, but I was not expecting to get it. Somehow my parents knew what I really wanted. I'll never forget opening up that first boxcar. I was so surprised that I was speechless. I couldn't believe they got me more than what I had asked for. Having your expectations blown away is one of life's greatest joys. And God does it all the time when we pray.

The Bible puts it this way, "Now to Him who is able to do far more abundantly beyond all that we ask or think, according to the power that works within us, to Him be the glory in the church and in Christ Jesus to all generations forever and ever."(Ephesians 3:20-21)

## GIVING US THE EXTRAS...

He gives us more than what we ask. In one of Jesus' final acts before His death He demonstrates this principle. A thief being crucified next to Jesus said, "Remember me when you come into your kingdom." (Luke 23:42) He just wanted a thought! Jesus responded by saying, "Today you will be with me in paradise!" (Luke 23:43) That's far more than a thought or even an honorable mention!

We need to stop praying like cynical adults who struggle to dream big dreams and pray big prayers. Instead, as noted author Paul Miller writes, "To learn how to pray is to enter the world of a child, where all things are possible."[1] When we recognize that God desires to give us more than we ask, our prayer lives will be radically transformed.

## GIVING US SOMETHING DIFFERENT

God often gives us something different than what we ask. Abraham experienced this in Genesis 18. He loved his nephew, Lot, who was living in Sodom. God told Abraham that He planned to destroy Sodom. So Abraham pleaded with God, "What if there are 50 righteous people in the city? Will You really sweep it away and not spare the place for the sake of the 50 righteous people in it?" And God says, "Okay." After Abraham thought about it he began to wonder if there were even 50 good folks there. So he said, "What if the number of the righteous is five less than 50? Will You destroy the whole city because of five people?" This bargaining process continued down to 10 righteous people. In reality, there were not even 10 righteous people in Sodom. So God did something different than Abraham asked. Instead of sparing the city, God sent two angels to rescue Lot and his family out of Sodom. Sometimes God answers our prayers by giving us something better or different.

---

1   Paul Miller, *A Praying Life.*

## GIVING US ENLIGHTENMENT

God also beats our expectations by opening our eyes to the truth. Sometimes we are praying for something physical when what we really need is spiritual enlightenment. This happened to Elijah. He defeated and killed the false prophets of Baal on Mount Carmel. However, just a few days later, Elijah was discouraged. He says:

"I have been very zealous for the Lord God Almighty. The Israelites have rejected Your covenant, broken down Your altars, and put Your prophets to death with the sword. I am the only one left, and now they are trying to kill me, too." (1 Kings 19:14)

He threw a pity party and invited God. I have done this many times. God responded to the invitation by enlightening him to the fact that 7,000 other people in Israel also had not bowed down to Baal. Sometimes God just opens our eyes to His truth and that is the answer to our prayer.

## GIVING US...HIMSELF

The greatest gift God offers is Himself. When you go to prayer, you actually meet God. The Bible says, "Be still and know that I am God." (Psalm 46:10) That's what prayer is all about; getting into God's presence, looking into His face through the eyes of your faith and just being still before Him. When we do this we understand the words of King David, "Better is one day in Your courts than a thousand elsewhere." (Psalm 84:10) That realization of God's presence changes everything. It is that "wow!" moment where everything else sort of melts away. All pride, selfish ambition, and wrong priorities vanish. God's presence changes and satisfies us.

So today let's pray expectantly – knowing that God will beat our expectations.

# DAY 6

*Why Pray? We Get God's Peace*

*"The peace of God, which surpasses all
understanding, will guard your hearts and your
minds in Christ Jesus."*
Philippians 4:7

*"Those persons who know the deep peace of God, the
unfathomable peace that passeth all understanding,
are always men and women of much prayer."*
*R.A. Torrey – Evangelist & Pastor 1800s*

Webster defines "nap" as a brief sleep, often during the day. I don't know about you, but I love a good nap. Nothing beats that feeling of rest that you get when you wake up. You're ready to go and conquer the world after a good nap. But the rest we get from a good nap does not even begin to compare to the rest we get when we come to God in prayer.

Jesus said, "Come to me, all you who are weary and burdened, and I will give you rest." (Matthew 11:28)

Weary and burdened – now those are words to which I can relate. Everyone has burdens. There are employment issues to worry about, bills that need to be paid, family members dying of cancer, kids who are unruly, and decisions we should not have made. Put them all together and you have a deadly concoction of a burdensome and weary life. But Jesus says it doesn't need to be that way. He says when we come to Him and we bring these burdens, we find rest.

## HOW DO I START?

"Well that all sounds good," you might say, "but how do I actually do that?" I think the prophet Isaiah offers some key insight for us. "You will keep in perfect peace those whose minds are steadfast, because they trust in you." (Isaiah 26:3) When you keep your mind and your focus on God, you get peace.

You might think that "tree skiing" is a stupid thing to do; you would only do that if you have a death wish. But there are skiers who love that virgin powder between the spruce trees and they love to tree ski. The key is, don't hit the trees! Tim Etchells talks about this in *Outdoor Magazine.* He says the key is to look between the spaces of the trees; "don't stare at what you don't want to hit." That's true in life. If you worry about things and focus on them, you will run right into them. But if your focus is on God, you will run right into Him.

We find rest when we set our gaze on Christ. In doing so we are reminded that we have been given everything we need for this life because of what Jesus has done on the cross. When we set our gaze on Christ we are reminded of God's goodness and His provision in our lives and we find rest in this truth, which allows the wearisome burdens to pale in comparison.

Adoniram Judson was a great Baptist missionary to Burma. He watched his wife and daughter die of the same disease within six months of each other. He saw extreme hostility to the gospel, and battled illness after illness but was still able to say shortly before his death: "I am not tired of my work, neither am I tired of the world." Judson found rest in his Savior, which trumped any hardship he experienced in his life.

## PRAYER REPLACES WORRY

The Apostle Paul tells us, "Do not be anxious about anything." (Philippians 4:6) Really Paul, anything? Indeed, Paul is saying not to worry about anything. That's pretty amazing because there are a lot of things to worry about – health, economics, relationships, concerns about your children – you have some big things you are facing right now. But the Bible says don't worry about anything. Then Paul uses another superlative. Those in the language business say not to use "all" and "every" – but the Bible does that here. "Do not be anxious about *anything*, but in *everything*, by prayer and petition, with thanksgiving, present your requests to God." (Emphasis added.) Turn the things that you are worrying about into prayers. You do have a choice in this life. Either you are going to worry, or you are going to pray – but you can't do both. You say, "No, I think I can. I can worry and pray at the same time." True prayer, though, releases these things to God and says, "Lord, I'm giving these things to You, trusting in You, and focusing on You after I've prayed." In other words, if you are really praying, your focus will be on God and not on the worry, particularly after your prayer.

## PEACE BEYOND UNDERSTANDING

Paul continues in the next verse, "and the peace of God, which transcends all understanding, will guard your hearts and your minds in Christ Jesus." (Philippians 4:7) He promises to guard your heart with His peace. Paul says the peace God will give you is beyond your understanding. I can tell you that I have sat with people who have gone through some horrific situations, yet God's peace dominates their lives. Humanly speaking, they should not have any peace, but God gives them peace. It's beyond understanding. Paul says prayer will "guard your heart." That word "guard" carries the idea of a Roman guard. He was not carrying pepper spray and a nightstick. He was a powerful man with a sword and he knew how to use it. God's peace is a powerful guard for your heart. Express your concerns to God, and then refuse to worry.

His peace will guard you. I hope today you will trust God's Word and refuse to worry.

Let's look at Paul's argument in reverse to see if that helps. Even though we are all sinners, God has made peace with us because of Christ's shed blood on the cross. That peace guards our hearts so we can be fully confident that we are accepted by God. So Paul says we can present all our requests to Him knowing that He cares for us and desires to meet our needs. And as a result, we don't have to worry about anything. Pretty cool huh? Learning why we pray means learning what the gospel says about God. And the gospel says that we have peace with God and therefore He will give us rest when we set our gaze on Him. Will you do that today? Will you pray and find rest in Jesus? It will transform you and give you a new outlook on your life. I guarantee that when you do it, you will enjoy some of the best naps you have ever had.

# DAY 7

*Why Pray? The End is Near*

> *"Therefore keep watch, because you do not know on what day your Lord will come."*
> Matthew 24:42

> *"Are we looking for our Savior's return? Do we long for His appearing? Can we say with sincerity, Come, Lord Jesus? Do we live as if we expected Christ to come again? These are questions which demand serious consideration. May we give them the attention which they deserve!"*
> J.C. Ryle – Anglican Bishop 1800s

If you knew that Jesus was coming back tonight, at midnight, what would you do today? How would you live this day if you knew that tonight Jesus Christ would return and we would be taken up into heaven? If you are like me, you would spend more time praying today than you probably did any other day of your life.

We are living in the last days, but we are not going to get a 24-hour countdown warning. We have to be ready every single day. Jesus said, "Therefore keep watch, because you do not know on what day your Lord will come." (Matthew 24:42) Since we do not know when Jesus is coming back, we need to keep short accounts with Him. We can't afford to have any offense lingering between God and us.

Jesus' last words in the Bible are these, "Behold, I am coming soon!" (Revelation 22:12) And if that is not enough, the second to last verse in the Bible is this "Yes, I am coming soon." These are the words of Jesus and He wants you to know something – He is coming back and He is coming back soon. There are at least three other reasons that we believe He is coming back soon.

## THE EXPLOSION OF KNOWLEDGE

"But you, Daniel, close up and seal the words of the scroll until the time of the end. Many will go here and there to increase knowledge." (Daniel 12:4) There will be a knowledge increase in the last days, and we are certainly experiencing that.

From the time of the Garden of Eden until the early 1900s, the transportation mode was a horse. King David, Alexander the Great, and George Washington rode a horse. In the early 1900s, the automobile was invented. Then it was an airplane, then a jet plane, then it was supersonic flight, and now you can get to Paris from New York in three hours! In less than 100 years, we went from a horse and buggy to travelling to the moon in a rocket. Talk about a knowledge increase!

Look at light – from the time of the Garden to the early 1900s, we were using torches and candles to light the way. Then the light bulb was invented and within 10 years nearly every household in America had light bulbs. Communication – from the time of the Garden of Eden until the early 1900s, we communicated using drums, smoke signals, even shiny pieces of brass and using the sun. Then the telegraph came into being, then the telephone, then the television, then the worldwide web; now my kids are watching Netflix on my iPhone (which explains why I can never find it). Knowledge is doubling every three years! We have seen an increase in knowledge in the last hundred years like the world has never known. This was predicted. "They will be...always learning but never able to acknowledge the truth." (2 Timothy 3:7) That describes our generation.

# THE REBIRTH OF THE NATION OF ISRAEL

On May 15, 1948, Israel was rebirthed as a nation. This rebirth was predicted almost 3,000 years earlier. "Who has ever heard of such a thing? Who has ever seen such things? Can a country be born in a day or a nation be brought forth in a moment? Yet no sooner is Zion in labor than she gives birth to her children." (Isaiah 66:8)

Jesus told His disciples that this event would be the sign of His coming. He did so by using the symbol of Israel, a fig tree:

> "Now learn this lesson from the fig tree: As soon as its twigs get tender and its leaves come out, you know that summer is near. Even so, when you see all these things, you know that it is near, right at the door. I tell you the truth, this generation will certainly not pass away until all these things have happened." (Matthew 27:32-34)

In other words, Jesus is saying, some of the people alive when Israel experiences her rebirth will physically see Him come. This is great news because my dad was born in 1948 and he is very old! That means Jesus' return can't be far off.

## MORAL DECAY

The last reason I believe Jesus is coming back soon is the moral decay that we are experiencing. Also in response to the question the disciples asked, Jesus says, "Because of the increase of wickedness, the love of most will grow cold..." (Matthew 24:12)

We are seeing this in our generation. You can turn on the news and hear about mothers who are suffocating and killing their babies. The natural love that people should have is in great decline and sin is increasing. The Bible predicted this.

"But mark this: There will be terrible times in the last days. People will be lovers of themselves, lovers of money, boastful, proud, abusive, disobedient to their parents, ungrateful, unholy, without love, unforgiving, slanderous, without self-control, brutal, not lovers of the good, treacherous, rash, conceited, lovers of pleasure rather than lovers of God – having a form of godliness but denying its power." (2 Timothy 3:1-5)

That describes pretty well the days in which we live. Jesus is coming back soon. It may happen in your lifetime. At the moment Jesus returns there is no more time to prepare – now is the time to prepare! Take time today and get ready for the coming of the Lord. Pray for your friends and family to be ready and to make their peace with God.

# week 2 | GETTING RESULTS

# DAY 8

*Getting Results - Praying in Faith*

*"You may ask me for anything
in my name, and I will do it."*
John 14:14

*"But go to Him when your need is desperate, when
all other help is vain, and what do you find? A door
slammed in your face, and a sound of bolting and
double bolting on the inside. After that, silence."*
C.S. Lewis – Author

When we pray, we want to get results. Oftentimes people pray and not a whole lot happens. John Piper says, "Unanswered prayer is a universal Christian experience."[1] One of the main focuses of *40 Days of Prayer* is to learn how to get real results with God.

The first thing you need to know is that we have to pray in faith. We can't pray and say, "Well, maybe it will happen, maybe it won't, but I'm going to ask God anyway." That's an insult to God! When we pray, we need to ask Him with confidence that He can do what we want Him to do. That's a compliment to God. The Bible says this over and over.

---

1  http://www.desiringgod.org/resource-library/sermons/what-do-answers-to-prayer-depend-on-part-1

The Bible says, "Let us then approach God's throne of grace with confidence, so that we may receive mercy and find grace to help us in our time of need." (Hebrews 4:16) Notice it says to approach the throne with confidence and that confidence is necessary so that we will receive answers to our prayers. Confidence is a necessary prerequisite for answers.

James talks about praying for wisdom and says when you need wisdom, just ask Him for it. "But when you ask, you must believe and not doubt, because the one who doubts is like a wave of the sea, blown and tossed by the wind. That person should not expect to receive anything from the Lord." (James 1:6-7) Remember that God hears everything you say and knows everything you think.

Imagine asking your boss for a raise, but somehow he knows you are constantly thinking, "I know he's not going to give me a raise, he's so stingy, he never gives me what I want." There is no way he'd give you the raise. So if you pray thinking, "Well, hopefully it will happen, but maybe not," God says don't even bother. You have to pray with your whole heart, with faith that God can do it and that He will do it.

## I'M NOT A SUPER CHRISTIAN

The first question I have is, "Why don't we believe? Why do we pray so often but we really don't believe?" I think one of the reasons we don't do that is because we say, "You know, I'm not a super Christian. I'm a Christian, but I'm not a super Christian, so maybe it's not going to happen for me." The Bible says, "Elijah was a human being, even as we are. He prayed earnestly that it would not rain, and it did not rain on the land for three and a half years." (James 5:17) When Elijah took his shirt off, do you know what was not there? A big red "S" on his chest. He was not a super Christian. He was just a follower of God, just like you and me.

# GOD IS TOO BUSY FOR ME

The second thing that comes to mind is, "God's too busy to answer my prayers. Why would God bother with me? I mean He does single-handedly run the whole universe, there is no way He has enough time to pay attention to little old me." You know, the Bible says that is exactly what God is in the business of doing – bothering with us, His children. And, by the way, when your children want something from you and you are able to give it to them, are they a bother to you? Or is it a joy to you to be able to give something to your children?

The Bible says, "Are not two sparrows sold for a penny? Yet not one of them will fall to the ground outside your Father's care." (Matthew 10:29) In other words, God in heaven knows when even a bird falls. He can keep that bird from falling if He really wants to. The point is, God is very concerned with your needs. By the way, in Luke 12, it says He knows how many hairs are on your head, and everyone else's head.[2] Now, if He knows that kind of detail about us, I think He cares about your needs and about my needs.

## I'M A HUGE SINNER!

Another common concern that comes up when we don't pray in faith is that we say, "Well, you know, I've sinned too much, so it might be that God is not going to be able to answer my prayers." Do you know that the Bible says that Paul, before he became a Christian, was actually in the business of killing Christians? That's what he did for a living. Moses also had committed a murder – and in both of those cases, do you know that God answered their prayers in huge, huge ways? As long as you ask God to forgive you for those sins of the past, you don't have to worry about them. They don't have anything to do with your prayer life right now.

---

2 The current world population is about 6.9 billion people and the average person has about 100,000 hairs on their head. That works out to be around 690 trillion different hairs, just on heads, that God is simultaneously aware of at any given time.

## WHAT DO I SAY?

Lastly, we don't pray in faith because we just are not in the practice of it. In other words, we aren't used to praying at all. So when a crisis comes, all of a sudden, we say, "I've got to pray!" And we don't know how. Many times I've stood in a hospital room with somebody and it's not a good scene because they are saying, "I don't even know how to pray. I have to pray for my husband who is not at all well and he might die, but I don't know how." That's really not God's will for our lives. It doesn't have to be that way. You can know how to pray. You can be in the habit of getting great results with God as you get in the habit of praying in faith.

This is not an isolated issue. There was a recent survey of pastors that was concerned with discovering what their various ministry emphases and priorities were. Sadly, prayer came in last, with only 3% of pastors listing it as a priority in their church.

## SO WHAT DO I DO?

There's a story in the Bible about a man who came to Jesus with his son who was demon-possessed. Oftentimes, the boy was falling into the fire or he was on the verge of drowning – this demon inside of him was trying to kill him. The father came to Jesus and this was the conversation – the dad asked Jesus, "But if you can do anything, take pity on us and help us." "'If you can'?" said Jesus. "Everything is possible for one who believes." Immediately the boy's father exclaimed, "I do believe; help me overcome my unbelief!" (Mark 9:22-24) If you don't have a lot of faith in God right now when you pray, you can ask for it. You can pray, "Lord, help me to overcome my unbelief. Help me to believe all the way."

# DAY 9

*Getting Results - Asking!*

> *"You do not have because*
> *You do not ask God."*
> James 4:2

> *"Asking is the beginning of receiving."*
> Jim Rohn – American Entrepreneur

Have you ever said to your child, "Use your words"? When kids are still in the process of learning how to verbalize what they want and need, they often have a tendency to fall back into the old pattern of just reaching for something, or making unintelligible squeaks and groans in hopes that you will magically know what it is they are thinking. They have to be taught and trained to bring their requests and needs to you verbally.

Oftentimes we treat God the same way. There is constantly a long list of things we want and need, but we prefer that God just go ahead and take care of them. He's God right? He knows everything that is going on and what I need. That's true, but that's not exactly how God works. He desires us to be part of the process. He wants us to bring our requests to Him so that we can learn to rely on Him as he meets our needs.

## BE SPECIFIC

Today we're going to look at asking. The way you can guarantee not to get results in prayer is to not ever ask. F.B. Meyer says, "The greatest tragedy of life is not unanswered prayer, but unoffered prayer."[1] Yesterday I heard a news report, and as I was thinking about it, I began to get very depressed. It was a report about the economy and just the general direction of our nation. So I talked to people about it, and the more I talked about it, the more depressed I became. I had to ask myself, "Why is it that I don't go directly to God with these things?" As I think about this question, I think there are three reasons why we don't go to God and ask Him in prayer for things that we need.

## A LACK OF FELLOWSHIP

The first reason is a big indictment on us. We simply are not in fellowship with God. The Bible says, "But if we walk in the light as He is in the light, we have fellowship one with another, and the blood of Jesus, His Son, purifies us from all sin." (1 John 1:7) If we are not doing what the Bible calls "walking in the Spirit," if we're not walking with Him on a day-by-day basis, things are going to come our way and knock us for a loop. And since we are not in the habit of talking to Him, we're not going to bring it before Him. We are just not in fellowship with Him.

## MY STUFF IS UNIMPORTANT

The second reason we are not asking is this – we don't want to bother God with little things. Why would God want my little stuff? But the Bible says, "Do not be anxious about anything, but in every situation, by prayer and petition, with thanksgiving, present your requests to God." (Philippians 4:6) Corrie Ten Boom said, "Any concern too small to be turned into a prayer is too small to be made into a burden." If you won't pray about it, then apparently it's not worth worrying about. And, by the way, it's not always the big things that knock us for a loop. Often it's the little things that pile up and pile up. As I thought about my life,

---

1 Fern Nichols. *Every Child Needs a Praying Mom*. Grand Rapids: Zondervan: 2003.

I thought about it not being one news report that bothered me – it was this thing going on and on, and pretty soon I was starting to get a little depressed.

## DOES IT MATTER?

There is a third reason why I believe we don't bring things before God. It is simply that we don't believe it will matter. We just don't think it's going to make a difference. We say to ourselves, "What can I do in the quietness of my own room that is really going to matter before God?" It does matter. Look at what the Bible says. Jesus says, "Ask and it will be given to you; seek and you will find; knock and the door will be opened to you." (Matthew 7:7) The apostle John puts it this way, "And if we know that He hears us – whatever we ask – we know that we have what we asked of Him." (1 John 5:15) Jesus also said, "And I will do whatever you ask in my name, so that the Son may bring glory to the Father. You may ask me for anything in my name, and I will do it." (John 14:13-14) These promises are not unqualified. "Lord let me win the lottery!" What we are asking for must be within God's desire. However, many things we lack are in the will of God, we just need to ask Him.

## THE RESULTS

What happens when we ask God for things? What is it that we actually get? Well, first, we get our needs met – that's what Jesus said, "I will meet your needs if you ask." The second thing that happens is, we get peace. The Bible says, "And the peace of God, which transcends all understanding, will guard your hearts and your minds in Christ Jesus." (Philippians 4:7)

## GET REAL SECURITY

We have peace and security when God meets our needs. Apart from God, there is no security. There is no financial security in this world. You don't have to listen to the news very long to hear of people who thought they were financially secure, losing that financial security. Just three years ago, during the financial crisis of 2008, there was a major spike in suicides. These men and women's security was in their money, so when they lost it, they lost their god; the thing that gave their life meaning and their life was now no longer worth living. So they ended it.[2] There is no health security. Without God, there is nothing that says you are going to wake up tomorrow morning, or even be okay. There is no relationship security. A lot of times we think, "I'm secure in my main relationships." But how many times have you seen a marriage break up after many, many years. The only security you will find is in God. When you ask Him to meet your needs, He gives you peace because you realize that everything you need, you find truly in the Lord.

## GET REAL JOY

Lastly, when we ask God, we get joy. Jesus says, "Until now you have not asked for anything in My Name. Ask and you will receive, and your joy will be complete." (John 16:24) Joy is simply happiness from within. All of us are looking for happiness. The most successful people in the world are continually looking for happiness. The person who says, "I pulled myself up by my bootstraps; I didn't need anything from God or anyone else," is a person looking for happiness. Maybe they did find a lot of success in this world, but didn't find happiness – because true happiness is only found in a relationship with Jesus Christ. A relationship where we can ask Him and receive from Him on a daily basis.

The bottom line is, if you're not asking, you're guaranteed not to get results with God. We have to ask. Why don't you ask Him for some things today? Why don't you tell Him what your needs are and experience having your needs met – a calming peace about your circumstances and the tremendous joy of getting closer to God.

---

2   http://www.huffingtonpost.com/2008/10/14/financial-crisis-suicide_n_134453.html

# DAY 10

*Getting Results - Giving God Your All*

*"Pour out your heart before him"*
*Psalm 62:8*

*"I do the very best I know how, the very best I can, and*
*I mean to keep on doing so until the end."*
*Abraham Lincoln – 16th President of the United States*

Most of us give everything when we go to work. We put our best foot forward because people are going to see the product that we produce. We put our best foot forward in public situations where people are going to see us. We also do that with our hobbies. We want to be the best we can be with our hobbies because we enjoy them. Solomon wrote, "Whatever your hand finds to do, do it with all your might." (Ecclesiastes 9:10) Surely this must include our conversations and relationship with God. Yet sometimes, we give minimal effort to prayer!

When it comes to praying, we say, "Oh, God, hey, I know that I'm in bed and everything else that is important has been done for the day, but before I go to sleep, I just wanted to say a couple of things to You." And then you address God again, "Oh Lord, bless the Cheerios, then the burger at lunch, then dinner…" And we wonder why our prayers are ineffective. Can you imagine if this was your relationship with your husband or wife? You say a sentence to her at most meals (unless you're in a hurry and forget) and then you give her about thirty seconds of your time as you're falling asleep. What a terrible relationship! In fact, that's not a relationship at all! Yet on some days, our prayer time is like that.

One morning when my daughter was three years old she had a fever, and our preschool did not take children with a fever. My wife worked in the office with me, so she brought Reilly in with her. Reilly laid down for a nap around 10 o'clock. She woke up an hour later and suddenly she began to go into convulsions. I yelled for Katie and she came into my office and we put some water on Reilly to help abate the fever. But she began to turn blue and stopped breathing. Of course, at the beginning of all this, we called 911. We did not know what else to do – but what we were doing was praying. I'll never forget my wife as she was calling out to God asking Him to save our child from dying. We didn't know if she was going to live – we really didn't know. Nothing like that had ever happened before. We never had a child of ours stop breathing and go just totally limp. The paramedics arrived quickly, but it seemed like forever. And by the end of the day, after spending some time at the hospital, Reilly was okay. But I must tell you, when we prayed over her in my church office, laying on the floor, it was pretty serious prayer. It was all we had inside of us – just praying, "God, save our daughter!" Now, I don't want to tell you that if you pray with everything that you have that God will answer your prayer every time. Because that doesn't always happen. People do die. Children die. We don't understand God's will. But I do know this, God wants us to pray with all of our hearts.

The Bible tells us how Jesus prayed, "During the days of Jesus' life on earth, he offered up prayers and petitions with loud cries and tears to the one who could save him from death, and he was heard because of his reverent submission." (Hebrews 5:7) He was not joking around in prayer. God the Father refers to this sort of prayer as "praying with all your heart." Jeremiah 29:12-13 says, "Then you will call on me and come and pray to me, and I will listen to you. You will seek me and find me when you seek me with all your heart."

## PRAYING EARNESTLY

What does it involve? First, it has to involve your heart. You need to really care about it if you are going to touch God's heart. When I was praying for my daughter's life, I was not apathetically praying like most of us do at night as we trail away to sleep, "Hey God, thanks for the day, and food, and that other stuff…" No! I was pouring out my heart and soul to God. That prayer was spirited with emotion.

It also has to involve humility. With all of your heart and all of your emotions, if you are going to pour out your heart to God, you are saying, "God, I cannot do it! I cannot affect this situation!" And, I'm telling you that when this happened with Reilly, I never felt more helpless in my whole life. There was nothing I could do. But when you cry out to God with all your emotions – that is an act of humility, and it touches God's heart.

Third, prayer must involve a priority change. When you need something from God, when that is all you are focused on, nothing else matters. When Reilly was lying on the floor, convulsing, the least of my worries was the economy. I didn't care about it. I didn't care who got elected president. I didn't care whether the house was clean or dirty, or any of the stuff that matters to me usually. All I thought about was my little girl.

## SOME EASY STEPS

Now, maybe you are saying, "I want to be where you are talking about; I want to have that emotion, I want to give it my all in prayer, but I don't know how. How do you make yourself feel?" There is something you can do that is an act of your will. It is a decision you make, apart from emotion that will provide you the emotion you need to get the results from God that you are seeking. Here's what Nehemiah the prophet did when he got bad news. "When I heard these things (bad news) I sat down and wept. For some days I mourned and fasted and prayed before the God of heaven." (Nehemiah 1:4) He fasted. One thing you can do is begin to fast. If you have a need in your life, something going on that is outside of your control and you need God to intervene, begin to fast. Your emotions will begin to kick in, you're going to be hungry and you will begin to realize you are making a cognitive decision that what you need from God is more important than eating. You will set aside the time you would normally take to eat and you pray. Every time you get hungry – pray. If you want to get results from God, you have to pray with passion. You have to give it your all.

So, feel confident about getting connected with God. There will be a day when you are with someone who needs prayer. Don't let that day come and not know how to reach God. Make it your practice. Make it your daily experience that exposes you to the heart of God.

# DAY 11

*Getting Results - Giving God Your ALL*

*"Lift up your hands in the sanctuary
and praise the LORD."*
Psalm 134:2

*"All to Jesus I surrender; all to him I freely give; I will ever
love and trust him, in his presence daily live."*
J. W. Van Deventer – Author of Hymn: I Surrender All

There is something that is almost never talked about. In fact, I've never heard a message on it in church. I've never even heard anyone talk about it. It is our posture in prayer. Do you remember the old praise and worship song, "Come Let Us Worship and Bow Down"? It was taken from Psalm 95:6 that reads, "Come let us worship and bow down, let us kneel before the Lord our maker." Notice that worship here is not just the words that we recite, it is a complete body exercise, it involves our posture, bowing down and kneeling. This has largely been ignored in churches today.

When you go to a football game, how do the fans act? Most fans are very excited. If you go to a 49ers game in San Francisco, they have their faces painted and their shirts off and they are painting "49ers" all over themselves; they're going crazy! They're on the edge of their seats, watching every play to see if the team is going to score. That's what fans do. But what do you think when you see someone at the game and they are just kind of sitting there, kind of bored – maybe they're playing a video game or reading the newspaper – just kind of sitting there? Is that a fan? Absolutely not! That person is uninterested in the game. It's about how they position themselves.

## ARE YOU ON THE EDGE OF YOUR SEAT?

The Bible tells us what Jesus sometimes did while praying. "Going a little farther, he fell with his face to the ground and prayed…" (Matthew 26:39) This was Jesus' position! Not just Jesus, though. This is what David did too. He says, "Come, let us bow down in worship, let us kneel before the Lord our maker…" (Psalm 95:6) Solomon did this while he was dedicating the temple. "He stood on the platform and then knelt down before the whole assembly of Israel and spread out his hands toward heaven." (2 Chronicles 6:13) Paul knelt and prayed while saying good-bye to some people he would never see again.

J. Vernon McGee recognized this when he wrote,

> "According to my humble judgment, the greatest need of the present-day church is prayer. Prayer should be the vital breath of the church, but right now it is gasping for air. One of the great Bible teachers of the past said that the church goes forward on its knees. Maybe one of the reasons the church is not going forward today is because it's not in a position to go forward – we are not on our knees in prayer."[1]

You might be saying, "Now wait a minute. Those were special occasions. So maybe you are just getting a little bit ahead of yourself." The special occasion was that they were in the presence of God! Here's how

---

1   J. Vernon McGee, *On Prayer: Praying and Living in the Father's Will*, Thomas Nelson: 2002.

special it was. Every day Daniel did it. The Bible says,

> "Now when Daniel learned that the decree had been published, he went home to his upstairs room where the windows opened toward Jerusalem. Three times a day he got down on his knees and prayed, giving thanks to his God, just as he had done before." (Daniel 6:10)

It wasn't just on special occasions; it was every day for him. Do you remember the movie Superman II from 1980? It was a great movie that contained an even greater, iconic scene. Superman had mysteriously disappeared and the invincible General Zod is taking over the world. He storms into the Oval Office and declares to the President his infamous line, "Kneel before Zod," and the President does. Kneeling is proper posture of respect when you are in the presence of a great power. Throughout history people have knelt before their earthly kings. How much more should we be willing to kneel before Jesus, the King of kings?

## WHY IS KNEELING IMPORTANT?

Now I'm not saying that you can't pray while you're driving. Or while you are lying down. You can. There are examples of that in the Bible, but this is here for a reason. There is a reason why the Bible is telling us they knelt down on their knees and prayed. Three things happen when you do that.

First, it humbles us. We are on our knees, on our face before God saying, "God, I'm nothing before You." This is one of the reasons kings sat on thrones. It elevated them above everyone else, above everyone who was inferior to them. No one was ever to be higher than the king. Being below the king was a sign that you were submissive to him and that he was superior to you. Today we demonstrate this to God by kneeling before him.

Secondly, it focuses us on prayer. There are a million other things I can focus on. If I'm sitting at my desk, I can be looking at my computer. I might have papers on my desk that I need to go through. But if I'm on my knees, I'm focused on one thing – no more distractions.

The third thing is that it guards us. It guards us from other people coming in and distracting us. When you see someone on their knees and they are praying, are you going to go in and say, "Hey, buddy, what time is it?" Of course not! You aren't going to bother that person.

## IS THIS THE ONLY WAY TO BE A FAN?

Now, if you are physically unable to get on your knees, you may be thinking, "You just aren't being sensitive at all to me." I get it. There's another option for you. Because the Bible also says, "Hear my cry for mercy as I call to You for help, as I lift up my hands toward Your Most Holy Place." (Psalm 28:2) "Arise, cry out in the night, as the watches of the night begin; pour out your heart like water in the presence of the Lord. Lift up your hands to Him…" (Lamentations 2:19) "I want men everywhere to lift up holy hands in prayer, without anger or disputing." (1 Timothy 2:8) So, if you can't get on your knees, lift up your hands to the Lord. If you can't lift up your hands, lift up your heart completely however you can.

It is said that 80% of communication is about what your body says. Whether you are on your knees, or with your hands in the air before God, you can give your all in prayer. My challenge to you today is that you give God your all. Pour out your heart to Him.

# DAY 12

*Getting Results - Praying in God's Will*

*"If we ask anything according
to his will, he hears us."*
1 John 5:14

*"The Third Petition of the Lord's Prayer is repeated
daily by millions who have not the slightest intention
of letting anyone's will be done but their own."*
Aldous Huxley – Author, Brave New World

ave you ever been to the mall around Christmas time? There is Santa Claus with little Johnny on his lap and he says, "Santa Claus, I want a pony." When it's Susie's turn, she says, "I want a Barbie." And Danny says, "I want a Lego castle." All these kids are asking Santa for what they want. Some of us look at God like that. We have this view of God that says we recognize that He is God and we really hope that He gives us what we want, but we don't have much of a relationship with Him. God is not a fat, jolly man with a bag of goodies. He is not a genie waiting for you to rub the lamp so He can give you what you want before He goes obediently back into the His little lamp. He is far more than that. He is a loving Father who will only give us what is best for us.

I want to tell you today how you can have all of your prayers answered. This is an important one. The Bible says,

> "This is the confidence we have in approaching God: that if we ask
> anything according to his will, he hears us. And if we know that he
> hears us – whatever we ask – we know that we have what we asked
> of him." (1 John 5:14-15)

Now there is one phrase in there that is really important, "according to His will." It is guaranteed as long as you ask "according to His will."

## GETTING YOUR HEART IN THE RIGHT PLACE

The key with this is to get our desires in line with God's plan and God's heart. David said, "Take delight in the Lord, and He will give you the desires of your heart." (Psalm 37:4) When you find your joy in God, your desires will be in line with His, and the Bible says, He will "give you the desires of your heart." Jesus says, "But seek *first* His kingdom and His righteousness, and *all these things* will be given to you as well." (Matthew 6:33 – emphasis added) "All these things" refers to the previous verses about food, clothing and shelter – life's basic necessities. God wants to give all of us good gifts, but God will not answer prayers that are ultimately going to harm us or take us further away from Him.

Now maybe you have had some unanswered prayers. Is it possible that you have been praying for things that were not in God's will? James describes praying with bad motives, "When you ask, you do not receive, because you ask with wrong motives, that you may spend what you get on your pleasures." (James 4:3) Are you praying for a nicer, newer car, a flat screen TV, a tropical vacation, or for your annoying mother-in-law to "go to be with the Lord?"

Even Aldous Huxley, the author of *Brave New World*, and outspoken critic of Christianity, recognized the importance of this aspect of prayer. He said, "The Third Petition of the Lord's Prayer (thy will be done) is repeated daily by millions who have not the slightest intention of letting anyone's will be done but their own."

## HIS WILL VS. OUR WANTS

Some of you right now are thinking, "Okay, I get it. That's the catch. It just wasn't God's will, so He's not going to do it for me." But you have to think of it like this. When I was 16 years old, I wanted a Mustang GT 5.0. My dad didn't get it for me, because he knew what I would do with that car. I would have had a lot of fun on the freeway and there is a good chance that I would have gotten hurt. In the same way, God is a far better father than any of us ever had. He will not give us something that is going to hurt us or is going to hurt our relationship with Him. You might get what you want, but it is not because God gave it to you. It's because you went out and took it. But God doesn't give us things that are going to hurt us.

A lot of times we ask for things that are going to hurt us in the long run, because we are asking for things we don't need today. As parents, we don't just go to Costco and buy a few giant boxes of food and dump them on our children. No, we feed them meal by meal, day by day. Part of the reason is that they then learn to trust and depend on us as their providers. In the same way, God says to ask for your daily needs – your daily bread – to get you through today. We say, "Lord, give me ten million dollars!" Why? "I never want to have to worry again." God says, "Yes, but you'll never have to pray again either. You think that you're going to get something, and then you won't need Me. Why would I give that to you? That's going to hurt our relationship."

Another thing we pray for that doesn't always get answered with a "yes" is when we pray that sick people get well. That's a great prayer. We ought to pray for that. There are many examples in the Scriptures of people praying for sick people to get better. Sometimes they did, and sometimes they didn't. Sometimes when we pray, sick people get better. Sometimes they continue to suffer or even die. But it isn't God's will to heal everybody. Our bodies are not designed to last forever. Take the apostle Paul for example. I think of all people, Paul would get his prayers answered. If there was ever a super Christian, it was Paul. He wrote two thirds of the New Testament. But look at what Paul says when bringing an unidentified physical problem before God. "Three times I pleaded with the Lord about this, that it should leave me. But he said to me, 'My grace is sufficient for you, for my power is made perfect in weakness.'" (2 Corinthians 12:8-9) God did not heal Paul, but used his weakness as an opportunity to draw Paul closer to Him.

There are many things I've prayed for in my Christian life – prayed for fervently – and God has said "No, this is not my will for you." And looking back, I'm glad. Those things I actually count as answered prayers. They weren't mistakes of God. He was withholding things that were bad for me, so I'm glad God said "no" to me. Today ask yourself – are your desires in line with God's will? Are you seeking Him first? Putting Him first before everything else in your life? Is He the source of your joy? Or are you asking for something that might drag you further and further away from a close relationship with Him?

# DAY 13

*Getting Results - Dealing with Different Results*

"*Shadrach, Meshach and Abednego replied [to the king]*
*'If we are thrown into the blazing furnace, the God*
*we serve is able to deliver us from it, and he will deliver us*
*from Your Majesty's hand. But even if he does not, we want*
*you to know, Your Majesty, that we will not serve your gods*
*or worship the image of gold you have set up.'"*
Daniel 3:16-18

"*Prayer is not overcoming God's reluctance,*
*but laying hold of His willingness.*"
Reverend Dr. Martin Luther

God always answers our prayers. However, He sometimes gives us different answers than what we expect to get. The first answer that we always get, almost every time, from God is – silence. Oswald Chambers writes, "You say, 'But He has not answered.' He has, He is so near to you that His silence is the answer. His silence is big with terrific meaning that you cannot understand yet, but presently you will."[1]

Remember the experience I shared earlier when my wife and I were on the floor of my office with our daughter who was not breathing. "Lord, please, please help her to breathe." And I was hoping for that one-second answer, but it didn't come. When she began to breathe,

---

1   John Cook. *The Book of Positive Quotations.* Minneapolis: Fairview Press, 2007, 201.

still she wasn't all better instantly. It took all day before she was getting back to normal. I wanted everything to be all better instantly. But that is where faith comes in. We have to believe that God will do what is best for us and for the world – and that He will do His will.

## ANSWERS FROM GOD

When you pray and there is only silence, you have to interpret God's answers. Actually, there are four answers I want to look at today. First, there is "yes." Yes is a great answer! I love to get that answer from God, then I can thank Him and move on.

However, that is not how it works every time. Sometimes, God says "yes, but…" I always worry about that "yes, but" because that means God is going to do what we ask Him to do; however, it may not turn out exactly like we thought it would.

A friend of mine just had this experience. She was praying about her job and asking God to work out this situation that was not going well, and God allowed her to be fired. This was not the answer she was looking for. The good news is that now she is in Christian service and able to really serve the Lord. Because He knows His plan, God does say, "yes, but" sometimes.

Sometimes God says "no." Now all of us have experienced this answer where God just says "no." This requires some interpreting. Maybe you have asked God for something that was not a good thing for you. Maybe you said, "Lord, I want to date that cute cheerleader." And God said "no." Then you look at the situation and realize, "Well, I'm a Christian and she isn't. Maybe it's best that it didn't happen."

Sometimes you pray for something and you have good motives and it is a good thing, but no dice. In the last chapter I mentioned Paul's thorn in his side. This "thorn" was keeping him from being extremely effective in ministry and God said "no." Jesus had the same experience. Three times Jesus said, "Father, are you sure about the cross?" In both cases, the argument can be made that it would have been better for Jesus not to die on a cross, or for the thorn to be removed from Paul's side. On the surface that makes sense, but deep down, God had bigger purposes. Paul said in this same passage, "This was to keep me from being conceited so God could really use me." And if Jesus had not died on the cross, there would be no salvation. So, sometimes God says "no" for a good reason.

Other times, God will say, "wait." That is what the Book of Job is about – waiting. Job just wanted to know why the Lord allowed almost every earthly thing he cared about to be taken away. Why are You allowing this? The Bible says, "Why did I not perish at birth and die as I came from the womb?" (Job 3:11) Why didn't I just die when I was born? Well, he did learn the answer. By the end of the Book of Job, he understood what had happened and he was able to see what God wanted to teach him through his suffering. Sometimes we never understand God's purposes and why He allows painful things.

# UNDERSTANDING GOD'S ANSWERS TO PRAYER

The Bible says the just shall live by faith. Faith in what, though? Faith in at least four things – the first is that God loves you. The apostle Paul writes, "He who did not spare his own Son, but gave him up for us all – how will he not also, along with him, graciously give us all things?" (Romans 8:32) God loves you. You can believe that. You can trust in that. Number two, you can believe that God acts in your best interest. Jesus said, "Which of you fathers, if your son asks for a fish, will give him a snake instead? Or if he asks for an egg, will give him a scorpion? If you then, though you are evil, know how to give good gifts to your children, how much more will your Father in heaven..." (Luke 11:11-13) When you buy gifts for your children, you don't get them junk that you know they will not want. No, you excitedly get them things that you know will give them joy. You desire to please them and give them good things. God is the same way, and so much more. He is going to give you the gift that is in your best interest.

Thirdly, you have to believe that God is smarter than you. Job says, "To God belongs wisdom and power; counsel and understanding are his." (Job 12:13) God is way smarter than us. So if He is telling us "no" or "wait," we just have to believe that He is going to do the best for us. Lastly, believe that some day God is going to reveal His plan to you. He is going to explain to you when you get to heaven why He did what He did. We have to live by faith, and sometimes we are going to get answers we don't expect from God. But these are also times that should cause us to praise God and thank Him for who He is and what He is doing in our lives.

God always answers prayer. Though it often seems that he doesn't, even a "no," or silence, is an answer. We need to remember that God always hears and responds to our prayers, even if we do not get exactly what we want. God is always paying attention, always listening. Be encouraged!

# DAY 14

*Getting Results - Praying in Jesus' Name*

*"I tell you the truth, my Father will give
you whatever you ask in my name."*
John 16:23

*"By Thee my prayers acceptance gain,
Although with sin defiled; Satan accuses
me in vain, And I am owned a child."*
John Newton – Anglican Clergyman 1700s

Have you ever heard someone say "in Jesus' Name, Amen?" Maybe you have said it. I've said it a thousand times. But have you ever wondered why we pray "in Jesus' Name, Amen?" Is it a special formula that gets what we want from God? Actually, the reason why we do this is very important.

## BIBLICAL INSTRUCTION

The first reason is that Jesus told us to pray this way. This alone should be reason enough for us to do it. Jesus said, "And I will do whatever you ask in my name, so that the Son may bring glory to the Father. You may ask me for anything in my name, and I will do it." (John 14:13-14) Again He says, "You did not choose me, but I chose you and appointed you to go and bear fruit – fruit that will last. Then the Father will give you whatever you ask in my name." (John 15:16) Jesus tells us how to pray. We pray to the Father, in His Name.

## HONOR THE ONE TRUE GOD

The second reason we are supposed to pray this way is that it identifies the Person to Whom we are praying. It identifies we are praying to the One true God. When your child is in trouble, or say they have had a nightmare, they do not just cry a general "Help!" in hopes some random person will save them. No, they cry out "Mommy!" or "Daddy!" They have a specific, trusted person in mind whose aid they desire. In the Old Testament, they would use the phrase, the God of Abraham, Isaac and Jacob. That's so we know we aren't talking about a false god. There are many false gods out there. In Arabic, the word "Allah" simply means god. So, how do you know you are talking about the One true God or about the false god, Allah? The way you distinguish is by description. You describe God by saying, "I'm talking to the One who sent Jesus, His only Son, to die for my sins." You're not talking about the god who sent the prophet Mohammed, who is not really a god at all. You're not talking about the god of Joseph Smith who presumably sent the angel Moroni to help him translate tablets. You're not talking about the god who is the force behind karma. You are talking about the One true God.

Paul dealt with this on Mars Hill. The Bible says, "Paul then stood up in the meeting of the Areopagus and said, 'Men of Athens! I see that in every way you are very religious.'" (Acts 17:22) They were very religious because they served "gods"– though not the One true God. Paul continues in the next verse, "For as I walked around and looked carefully at your objects of worship, I even found an altar with this inscription: to an unknown god…" He says, "That's the one you've been missing!" and Paul begins to describe who He is.

## BE CAREFUL

If you are praying in general to a god, don't be under the illusion that you are praying to the One true God. In fact, the Bible is a chronicle of God's anger against false gods and His acts against false gods, who really are not gods at all. Michael Horton similarly argues "the entire Bible can be construed as a long court case of Yahweh versus the Idols, with God's image bearers as his witnesses."[1] God is not some higher power, a mystic force, or a vortex. If you are praying to that kind of god, you can expect no results at all. God is a loving heavenly Father who wants to have a relationship with us. He sent His Son, Jesus Christ, to die on a cross for our sins. And so we pray, "In Jesus' Name, Amen."

## CHARACTER COUNTS

The third reason why we pray "in Jesus' Name" is because it identifies the character, the authority and the reputation of the One to whom we are praying. You see, a name is more than just a title in the Bible. It is a description of character. God changed Jacob's name from Jacob, which meant "deceiver" to Israel, which meant "prince of God," because his character changed. God changed Peter's name. He changed Abram's name from Abram, which meant, "father" to Abraham, which meant "father of many." God's Name is perfect. This is why Jesus says, "hallowed be Thy Name," as He teaches us to pray. We are supposed to lift up God's Name.

The Bible does this over and over. David says, "O Lord, our Lord, how majestic is Your Name in all the earth!" (Psalm 8:1) His name is His character, and that is why we pray, "In Jesus' Name." The Bible says,

> "Therefore God exalted Him to the highest place and gave Him the Name that is above every Name, that at the Name of Jesus every knee should bow, in heaven and on earth and under the earth,

---

1  Michael Horton. *The Christian Faith*. Grand Rapids: Zondervan, 2011. 132

and every tongue confess that Jesus Christ is Lord, to the glory of God the Father." (Philippians 2:9-11)

It is because the Name of God is great that we pray "in Jesus' Name."

## GIVING GLORY TO GOD

The fourth reason we pray "in Jesus' Name" is that it reminds us that we need to pursue God's interests, Jesus' interests, Jesus' kingdom, in prayer; that we are looking for God's glory, not our own trifle interests and things that we would want for our own personal gratification.

We need to remember that when we pray, we are approaching God. And we can only do this because of the shed blood of Jesus. So, we pray in Jesus' Name because it is only through Jesus that we have access to God. He is our great high priest who is continually interceding for us with God the Father. Through His death, He tore down the veil separating us from God. John Piper puts it like this,

> "Nobody gets an answer to prayer by asking God for it without depending on Jesus Christ. Christ is the One who, by his blood and righteousness, has purchased for sinners every blessing in the heavenly places. Therefore every prayer I pray is 'In Jesus' Name,' meaning 'based on Jesus' death and righteousness as the One who purchased every blessing that I will ever obtain.'"[2]

---

2  http://www.desiringgod.org/resource-library/ask-pastor-john/should-i-pray-in-jesus-name-when-asked-to-pray-in-public

# week 3 | MEETING GOD

# DAY 15

*Meeting God - Your First Meeting*

*"At once he began to preach in the synagogues that Jesus is the Son of God. All those who heard him were astonished and asked, 'Isn't he the man who raised havoc in Jerusalem among those who call on this name?'"*
Acts 9:20-21

*"You must picture me alone in that room at Magdalen, night after night, feeling, whenever my mind lifted even for a second from my work, the steady, unrelenting approach of Him whom I so earnestly desired not to meet. That which I greatly feared had at last come upon me. In the Trinity Term of 1929 I gave in, and admitted that God was God, and knelt and prayed: perhaps, that night, the most dejected and reluctant convert in all England."*
C.S. Lewis – Author

Life is full of important meetings. Take for example, the meeting that took place on July 4, 1776, where 56 men gathered to declare independence from the British Empire. Or consider the meeting that effectively ended the most horrific war in U.S. history, which took place in 1865 on the Appomattox Court House steps between legendary generals Robert E. Lee and Ulysses S. Grant.

Your life is not exempt from important meetings either. There's the first time you met the person you would marry (or the first time you met your in-laws). There are meetings for work, PTA meetings, meetings at church. Life is full of important meetings, but none more important than when we meet with God in prayer. Have you ever thought of prayer that way? Prayer is just that – a meeting with God.

## SPENDING TIME WITH GOD

The best part of prayer is not the stuff that God gives you; it's not even the answers to prayer. The best part of prayer is meeting God; spending time in the presence of God. A lot of people miss this; they miss the point of life. Take for example, the point of heaven. A lot of people think that the joy of heaven will be the streets of gold, or the crystal sea, or the mansions. Baloney! The joy of heaven is the presence of God, being with Jesus.

Philip Yancey writes, "The main purpose of prayer is not to make life easier, nor to gain magical powers, but to know God. I need God more than anything I might get from God." Think of it this way – when we pray we meet with God. And when we meet with God, we get to know Him better. It's like your spouse or a good friend. You long to meet with them. Why? So that you can know them better. It's the same with God. Prayer offers us the opportunity to meet with God and to know Him in an intimate and personal way.

## BEING TRULY REPENTANT

I want to focus on your first meeting with God. Your first meeting with God has to start differently than those that follow. You see, you are born with a problem. You are born spiritually dead. God told Adam and Eve, "The day you eat of this fruit, you will surely die." And they did. And all their offspring died, spiritually. The Bible says, "As for you, you were dead in your transgressions and sins…" (Ephesians 2:1) That's how you were born – spiritually dead. So this has to be rectified. God is not your Father when you were born. Jesus went as far as saying, "You belong to your father, the devil, and you want to carry out your father's desire." (John 8:44)

## BORN A SINNER

That's why the world is like it is. God is not your God when you are born; not until you receive Him and accept Him. The Bible teaches that Satan is the god of this world. So, in your first meeting with God, you have to make peace with Him. This paves the way for the rest of your relationship. Now, a lot of people miss this step and they wind up with a religion and not a relationship. All the time I hear people say, "I must be okay with God because I pray every night before I go to bed." The fact that they pray every night before going to bed does not mean that they have hit that first step and are actually reconciled to God. This has to happen by blood. The Bible says that without the shedding of blood there is no remission of sins. You see, you cannot turn the clock back and say, "I know I've disobeyed Your laws, God, but I still want to be holy, so I'm just getting in this time machine and turning the clock back." You can't do that. There had to be a sacrifice.

## TAKING CARE OF SIN

The Bible describes the sacrifice of Jesus, even before it happened, in Isaiah 53:5, "But he was pierced for our transgressions, he was crushed for our iniquities; the punishment that brought us peace was upon him, and by his wounds we are healed."

The punishment that will bring you peace with God was upon Jesus. He paid for us to be reconciled to God, to be okay with God, not to be enemies of God anymore. That was on Jesus. Because He did that, we have to accept Jesus. We can't just accept Him as a historical fact. That's getting religion. You need to accept Him as your Savior. The way you do this is to say this, "I don't want my old life anymore; I want a new life – a new life with Jesus." That's called repentance. Jesus said, "unless you repent, you too will all perish." (Luke 13:3,5) We have to repent. When you do that, you are accepting Him by faith. The Bible says, "And without faith it is impossible to please God, because anyone who comes to him must believe that he exists and that he rewards those who earnestly seek him." (Hebrews 11:6)

You have to believe and accept Him by faith. What words would you use to do this? The Bible teaches us exactly what to say. "That if you confess with your mouth, 'Jesus is Lord,' and believe in your heart that God raised him from the dead, you will be saved. For it is with your heart that you believe and are justified, and it is with your mouth that you confess and are saved."(Romans 10:9-10)

You are saying, "Jesus, You are Lord. You are on the throne, and I want You to be my Lord." Have you ever called on His Name? Have you ever asked Him to forgive your sins and come into your life and change you and give you a new life?

My guess is that as you're reading this you either have several important meetings to go to today, or you've already been in several important meetings. But don't pass up the opportunity for the most important meeting you'll ever have. I invite you to pray – to meet with God and ask Him to save you from your sin. You can pray something like this…

"God in heaven, thank You for sending Jesus to die on the cross for my sins. I receive Him as my Lord and Savior. I ask that You will come into my life, forgive my sins and give me a new home in heaven. Thank You for loving me. In Jesus' Name. Amen." If you made that decision, today is the first day of the rest of your life; the first day of meeting God. Congratulations, and welcome to the family of God.

That is your first meeting with God and it paves the way for the rest of your relationship with Him, for all eternity.

Today as you pray I challenge you to approach God with a heart to know Him more. Don't be so consumed with what you get out of it. Rather go and meet with Him for the sake of being with Him.

# DAY 16

*Meeting God - Walking with God*

> *"He has told you, O man, what is good; and what does the LORD require of you but to do justice and to love kindness, and to walk humbly with your God."*
> Micah 6:8

> *"To walk with God is to walk after the Spirit – to look to the Holy Spirit as our Teacher, to lean on Him for strength, to put no confidence in the flesh, to set our affections on things above, to wean them from things on earth, and to be spiritually-minded."*
> J.C. Ryle – Anglican Bishop 1800s

I can remember the walks on the beach that Katie and I took before we got married. There was a particular area called The Strand, Manhattan Beach, Hermosa Beach and Redondo Beach in Southern California. We loved taking long walks on the beach – not for exercise, but to spend time together. In fact, that's where I proposed to Katie.

God is inviting you to go on a walk with Him. It's a walk with Him through good times, through bad times, through sickness, through health – even through the "valley of the shadow of death," when you close your eyes to this life and open your eyes to see Him, face to face. It is a walk that will continue through eternity.

# DEVELOPING A RELATIONSHIP

Walking with God is not so much concerned with theology but with friendship. Theology is very important; it tells us who God is. But prayer allows us to move beyond that to a place where no creeds or doctrines could take us.

Walking with God will set you apart from this world. Most people live ordinary lives. They strive to make money, to raise a family, to retire, and then eventually die. That's it. That was not God's purpose in creating you. He wants you to walk with Him. That is exactly what the Bible says that Enoch did. In fact, the Bible says that he walked so closely with God that one day, "He was no more." In other words, God just took him to heaven. That even beats dying in your sleep!

The Bible says Noah walked with God and did extraordinary things for God; he was extremely different from everyone else who was living in his time. It was a very wicked time, yet there was this one guy who was walking with God – not just living, but also walking with God. What does it mean to walk with God?

The Bible tells us that we, too, can walk with God. Paul says, "So I say, walk in the Spirit, and you will not gratify the desires of the sinful nature." (Galatians 5:16) Over and over again we are told to walk in the Spirit. The apostle John puts it this way, "But if we walk in the light, as he is in the light, we have fellowship with one another, and the blood of Jesus, his Son, purifies us from all sin." (1 John 1:7) Jesus says, "I am the vine; you are the branches. If a man abides (Lives) in me and I in him, he will bear much fruit. Apart from me you can do nothing." (John 15:5)

# DEEPENING YOUR RELATIONSHIP

Eight times Jesus says to "abide in me" or "live in me." How do we do this? Again, what does it mean to walk with Jesus or walk with God? There is a passage in John 10 that gives us three important clues on how we can deepen our relationship with God, and how we can abide with Him. "The watchman opens the gate for him, and the sheep listen to his voice." (John 10:3)

## LISTEN FOR HIS VOICE

The first thing you have to do if you are going to walk with God is be sensitive to His voice. The Bible teaches us that when we accept Jesus as our Lord He gives us the Holy Spirit, and He comes as our Comforter, but also to be our Guide. He leads us into truth. We need to listen to the voice of the Spirit.

## OBEY HIS VOICE

The second clue here is that we need to obey His voice. Jesus continues by saying, "When he has brought out all his own, he goes on ahead of them, and his sheep follow him because they know his voice." (John 10:4)

It is not enough just to *hear* God's voice, we also need to *obey* God's voice. If God is walking one way and we go off another way, then we are not walking with God anymore. Keep in mind that the Bible says Enoch and Noah walked with God; the Bible does not say that God walked with them. In the same way, we must follow His lead; He doesn't follow our lead. We don't make plans and then say, "Oh, would you bless these plans?" We say, "Lord, what would you like the plan to be?"

## TRUST GOD

The third feature here is that if we are going to walk with Him, we have to trust Him. Jesus said, "I am the good shepherd. The good shepherd lays down his life for the sheep." (John 10:11) This is why the sheep follow the shepherd. They know that if a wolf sneaks into the pack, a hired hand isn't going to risk anything for those sheep. But the shepherd will lay down his life for them. So the sheep follow him. We have to trust that God has our best interests at heart. When we do that, we begin to trust Him enough to follow Him.

My dog loves me and trusts me with his life. He would do anything for me. So when I say, "Hey, Pauly, come get in the car!" Pauly flies into the car, and he doesn't have to know where we're going. We might be going to the vet to get his teeth cleaned, or something that he doesn't really like. But he trusts me; he wants to be with me.

Remember that prayer encompasses listening, obeying, and trusting God's voice. Since prayer is intimate communication with God it creates sensitivity towards God's voice. Furthermore, it opens our hearts to being obedient because we learn to trust Him more. This is how the relationship with God deepens. This is called walking with God. Just as I enjoyed those walks with my wife talking to her and getting to know her better, the rest of your life can be spent walking with God, and enjoying Him forever.

I challenge you to walk with God, not merely talk with God – to pray *with* Him not merely *to* Him. And enjoy the beauty of getting to know Him in the most personal relationship you'll ever experience.

# DAY 17

*Meeting God - Expect Your Faith to Grow*

*"Truly, I say to you, if you have faith like a grain of mustard seed, you will say to this mountain, 'Move from here to here,' and it will move, and nothing will be impossible for you."*
*Matthew 17:20*

*"O, when it comes to faith, what a living, creative, active, powerful thing it is. It cannot do other than good at all times."*
*Reverend Dr. Martin Luther*

We've already looked at how prayer demonstrates our need for God. Today we're going to look at how prayer demonstrates our faith in God. When we face situations in life that seem desperate, we all ask ourselves, "What are we going to do?" But how many of us think to pray?

## FROM NEED TO FAITH

The question is, what do you do when the bottom falls out? If you have your faith firmly planted in God, His providence and His ability to take care of you, you go right to Him.

First, let's look at what we mean when we talk about faith. The Bible defines faith this way, "Now faith is the assurance of things hoped for, the conviction of things not seen." (Hebrews 11:1) Thus faith is believing in something that we can't see. Believe it or not, we use faith every day – whether we believe in God or not.

When you receive a paycheck from your employer, you get a check – not actual greenbacks. You put that check in the bank. But you don't see it. You believe that the tellers and accountants will keep an accurate record of your deposits. That is faith.

The Bible gives many examples of men and women who did extraordinary things because of their faith in God. Hebrews 11 has been called the "hall of faith" because it lists so many biblical heroes. One of these heroes was Noah. The Bible says:

"By faith Noah, when warned about things not yet seen, in holy fear built an ark to save his family." (Hebrews 11:7)

God had told Noah that He was going to flood the earth. He told Noah to build an ark to save the animals and his family. Noah believed God because he had met with God. Now, why is it that when you meet with God, your faith grows? I think there are several reasons why that happens.

## GROWING FAITH

First, because God meets our needs. Over and over when that happens in your prayer life, you get more faith, more faith and more faith. George Mueller was a man who planted many orphanages for the kingdom of God, and he kept a journal of his prayer requests. There were over 10,000 answers to prayer in his journal. Not one request went unanswered. Our faith grows when we see God meeting our needs.

Shortly after the Dallas Theological Seminary was founded in 1924, it was on the verge of bankruptcy. Creditors were about to foreclose on the seminary at noon one particular day. That morning a group of men met in Dr. Chafer's office; he was the president of the Seminary, and one of those men was Dr. Harry Ironside. He prayed in his characteristic way, saying, "Lord, we know you own the cattle on a thousand hills. We pray you will sell some of them and send us the money." Well, not too long after that, a tall Texan in boots and an open-collared shirt walked into the business office. He said, "I just did a business deal and sold two carloads of cattle in Fort Worth. I was trying to close the deal, but it fell through. I felt compelled to come here and give you some money. I don't know whether you need it, but here it is." The secretary timidly knocked on the door where the prayer meeting was going on. Dr. Chafer answered the door and she said, "Here's a check that just came in from a Fort Worth cattle rancher." He took the check and it was for the exact amount they were praying for! Harry Ironside was still praying and Dr. Chafer tapped him on the shoulder and said, "Harry, God just sold the cattle." How many times does that have to happen to you before you say, "God can take care of my needs. He can handle my problems."

## YOUR PERSPECTIVE CHANGES

Secondly, our faith grows when we meet with God because He gives us peace, regardless of our circumstances. As previously noted, the Bible says, "Do not be anxious about anything, but in everything, by prayer and petition, with thanksgiving, present your requests to God. And the peace of God, which transcends all understanding, will guard your hearts and your minds in Christ Jesus." (Philippians 4:6 -7)

When you get that peace that God promises you, your faith grows. If you get a statement in the mail regarding your IRA, and you see significant losses, you may go to God in prayer because you are in trouble. You know what won't change? The situation. You'll look at that statement after you pray and it will say the same thing. But you will be different. Once you pray and you get God's peace, you will trust that God will meet your needs in a way other than that piece of paper. When you get that peace, your faith grows. That peace changes your perspective.

# GOD MATURES US

The third reason why your faith grows when you meet with God is because God changes us through prayer. How many times have you gone to the Lord in prayer feeling fear, a sense of loss, selfishness, anger, strife, bitterness, or greed? Yet after you have been in the presence of God, you've walked away with something entirely different. You've walked away with the fruit of the Spirit.

This "fruit of the Spirit" is this: "Love, joy, peace, patience, kindness, goodness, faithfulness, gentleness, and self-control." (Galatians 5:22)

Those are not things you can fake on the inside. You can only get them from God. And when you get them, you are maturing as a Christian, hence your character changes. As you change, your faith grows. You know God is real. You know you are not just doing yoga or meditating. You are in the presence of God and you know it because you are changed on the inside.

When we face difficulty we have to ask ourselves, "What do we do?" I would suggest there's nothing better than to pray. Prayer gives us faith that God will meet our needs. Subsequently we grow in faith as we see God meet these needs. So will you pray in faith today? And when you do, expect your faith to grow.

# DAY 18

*Meeting God - Your Light Intensifies*

> *"Let your light shine before others,*
> *so that they may see your good works*
> *and give glory to your Father who is in heaven."*
> *Matthew 5:16*

> *"Walking in the light is the opposite of walking in dark-*
> *ness. It means seeing reality for what it is and being*
> *controlled by desires that accord with God's light. If*
> *God is light, and in Him is no darkness at all, then he is*
> *the bright pathway to the fulfillment of all our deepest*
> *longings. He is the deliverer from all dark dangers and*
> *obstacles to joy. He is the infinitely desirable One."*
> *John Piper – Author, Desiring God*

Point Sur is a National Historic Landmark; the only complete turn-of-the-century light station open to the public in California. From 1899 until 1974, it served the Big Sur Coast.

Every time I see the lighthouse, I am reminded of its purpose. Yes, it is beautiful and, yes, the history is interesting. But I never forget its purpose, which is to warn ships of impending danger and to steer them in a better direction. This is what we're called to do as Christians when Jesus says, "You are the light of world." As Christians we carry the good news of the gospel to warn people of impending danger (hell) and steer them in a better direction (Jesus).

## MAKING OUR LIGHT BRIGHTER

Prayer is one of the essential ways in which we allow our light to shine brighter. And today we're going to look at how.

Have you ever had one of those lights in your house with a dimmer switch? The more you turn that knob up, the brighter it gets. In the same way, the more you meet with God, the brighter your light becomes.

This is how prayer causes our light to shine brighter, as we meet with God in prayer we become more deeply connected to the source of our light and thus it grows brighter. "This is the message we have heard from him and declare to you: God is light; in him there is no darkness at all." (1 John 1:5)

## TWO LIGHTS

God is light in two ways. First, He is physical light. When Paul was on the road to Damascus, what hit him? What knocked him down? It was a bright light coming down from heaven. When Moses came down from the mountain, having met with God, his face was bright because of the glory of God shining on him. At the Mount of Transfiguration, a few of the disciples were with Jesus, and God the Father came down in a cloud of light and spoke to them. Revelation chapter 21 describes heaven as having no need of light because God's glory is its light.

Second, God is spiritual light. We talked before about meeting with God and our faith growing because we get changed. Why is that? Why do we get changed, and how is light infused into us? That happens because in the presence of God, you get spiritual light. Jesus said, "I am the light of the world. Whoever follows me will never walk in darkness, but will have the light of life." (John 8:12) When you get into His presence, you get light. Jesus also said, "I have come into the world as a light, so that no one who believes in me should stay in darkness." (John 12:46) He says, "stay in darkness" because the world is full of darkness. We used to live in darkness, but now we have the light of Jesus and His word.

How can we live as children of light? There is an old song that says, "Turn your eyes upon Jesus, look full in His wonderful face; and the things of earth will grow strangely dim in the light of His glory and grace." The writer of Hebrews says, "Let us fix our eyes on Jesus." How do we look to Jesus? You think about Jesus. You spend time with Him in prayer. And when you do that, He is going to shine light in your life.

Think about it as a suntan. The more time your skin is exposed to the sun the more your skin reflects that exposure. So if you're like me, the more time you spend in the sun the redder your skin gets. When you see people in the summer you can tell how much time they've spent out in the sun working or sun bathing. The same "time of exposure" is true for us as Christians.

## TIME WITH GOD RESULTS IN GREATER REFLECTION

The more time we spend with God in prayer, the more it reflects in our lives, and we reflect that exposure. We will always look different when we spend time with God. And people around us will not be able to miss the change that is taking place in us.

There are three areas where He will shine light in your life. The first is that He shines light onto His own Word. "Your word is a lamp to my feet and a light for my path." (Psalm 119:105) How do we get that Word? How do we understand the Word? What illuminates it? The Bible says that God does that. "Open my eyes that I may see wonderful things in your law." (Psalm 119:18)

David is praying for God to open his eyes. When you meet God, you are in the presence of the Author of the Bible! What better person to ask about His word? This is why when you read the Bible, you should always pray. I always pray before I read the Bible, saying, "Lord, open my eyes so I can behold wonderful things from Your word." It's a great prayer from the lips of David. God will shine light onto His word, and you will get light for your own life.

Second, He shines light on us. We see ourselves as God sees us, when we get into His presence. This happened with Isaiah. Look at Isaiah 6:5, where he is in the presence of God and it is a great thing – and he says, "Woe to me!" I cried. "I am ruined! For I am a man of unclean lips, and I live among a people of unclean lips, and my eyes have seen the King, the LORD Almighty."

He was a wreck! He was in the presence of God and when he looked at himself, he realized that compared to God, he was nothing! When we see ourselves in a new light, we are humbled.

The third way that He shines light on us when we meet with Him, is that He shines light on other people. We see them as God sees them. Jesus loved them enough to put His life on the line and die for them. When we see people as He sees people, we will love them.

"Anyone who claims to be in the light but hates his brother, is still in the darkness. Whoever loves his brother lives in the light, and there is nothing in him to make him stumble." (1 John 2:9 & 10)

When you get into the light, you will see people a lot differently. Yes, people are imperfect. People offend you, people hurt you – sometimes even intentionally. But when you look at others with God's glory and His presence shining on them, you see them differently and you can love them.

I encourage you today to meet with God, get into His light and let it shine on your world. Get out your sunglasses!

# DAY 19

*Meeting God - Your Perspective Changes*

*"Give thanks to the Lord, for He is good, for His steadfast love endures forever."*
Psalm 136:1

*"We pray for the big things and forget to give thanks for the ordinary, small (and yet really not small) gifts. How can God entrust great things to one who will not thankfully receive from Him the little things?"*
*Dietrich Bonhoeffer – German Theologian & Martyr*

Have you ever received an awesome gift from someone? I know I have. What's your first response? Well if you're anything like me, it's gratitude. You just want to grab the giver and hug them until they pop.

It has been said, "Gratitude is the parent of all virtues." Tony Robbins, a self-help guru who sometimes stumbles onto biblical truth, made gratitude "the beginning of his day." Those who follow this guru are supposed to spend the first five minutes of their day being thankful for what they have, although Mr. Robbins doesn't make it clear who they should thank.

What happens when you are grateful? According to *Web MD*, when you are grateful, you reduce the stress in your life. It says that stress is linked to nearly every leading cause of death, including heart disease and cancer. Stress is responsible for 90% of doctor visits. When you are grateful, *Web MD* says your immune system gets a boost. It helps everyone, from people with AIDS to people going through surgery. Yes, there are a number of benefits to being grateful.

## PROPER EXERCISE, YOUR GRATITUDE MUSCLE

If I told you that prayer makes us more grateful, would you believe me? It does. And Jesus shows us how in Matthew 7:7-12:

> "Ask, and it will be given to you; seek, and you will find; knock, and it will be opened to you. For everyone who asks receives, and the one who seeks finds, and to the one who knocks it will be opened. Or which one of you, if his son asks him for bread, will give him a stone? Or if he asks for a fish, will give him a serpent? If you then, who are evil, know how to give good gifts to your children, how much more will your Father who is in heaven give good things to those who ask him! So whatever you wish that others would do to you, do also to them, for this is the Law and the Prophets."

Do you see that two-letter word "so" at the beginning of verse 12? This is the key to the passage. Essentially Jesus is saying that when we pray persistently we begin to see how God is a loving Father who gives us the good things that we desire. The word "so" indicates that when we understand God's love, evidenced through prayer, we will love others and express gratitude in the way we interact with them.

Tony Robbins has a good idea about starting each day with gratitude. But it is futile if we are not expressing that gratitude toward the One who is worthy of our thanks. This is why David says, "Let us come before him with thanksgiving and extol him with music and song." (Psalm 95:2) This is a great way to start your time with the Lord. But gratitude grows also because we become thankful for God's amazing acts; not only in our lives, but in other peoples' lives. "Hallelujah! I want to express publicly before his people my heartfelt thanks to God for his mighty miracles. All who are thankful should ponder them." (Psalm 111:1 – Living Bible)

## BEING THANKFUL

You need to go into the presence of God with gratitude for the things He has done in your life and throughout history. What has God done in your life for which you have not thanked Him? Maybe some answers to prayer have come your way and you haven't really taken much time to thank God. These are things you ought to bring before God every day. It changes our perspective. On one occasion Jesus healed 10 lepers, but only one of them thanked Him. Can you imagine being one of the nine whose lives were changed, but never said thank you?

Psalm 40:16 gives the greatest reason why we ought to be thankful to God, "May all who come before you be glad and joyful. May all who are grateful for your salvation always say, 'How great is our God!'" Have you thanked God for your salvation? Have you said, "Lord, without you, I would literally be lost. I would be on my way to hell with no idea where the Light is." How much time do you spend thanking God for your salvation? That's something to add to your daily time with Him.

## CHANGED PERSPECTIVE

Lastly, when you pray in gratitude and give thanks to God in your circumstance, it changes your outlook. Your outlook changes because you realize you are not a victim, you are a victor. You can always be thankful. If fact, the Bible says, "Give thanks in all circumstances..." (1 Thessalonians 5:18)

When Robinson Crusoe was shipwrecked on an island off the coast of Africa, he made a list. On one side he wrote the word "Evil" and on the other side he wrote "Good." On the evil side he wrote, "I'm all alone." On the good side he wrote, "I'm alive." Evil side, "I don't have any clothes." Good side, "It's a hot climate, don't really need clothes." Evil side, "I have nothing to defend myself with." Good side, "It doesn't appear that there are any wild beasts here to harm me." Point by point, Crusoe found something to be thankful for. There were lots of evil things, but good things offset these.

There's an area in Mexico where natural hot springs are found right next to natural cold springs. One tour guide was showing some visitors the springs and commenting that the women of the area would come to wash their clothes there because they could use the hot springs for washing, and the cold springs for rinsing. One of the tourists commented, "These women are probably so grateful to Mother Nature for providing this." The tour guide said, "Actually, they're not. Unfortunately they grumble a lot because Mother Nature didn't provide any soap." You can spend the rest of your life upset with God because He doesn't provide "soap," or you can thank Him for the "hot and cold springs." It just depends on your outlook. The more you meet with God, the more grateful you are going to be.

The great 19th century preacher Charles Haddon Spurgeon said:

> "I want to urge you, dear friend, to observe the goodness of God carefully for your soul's good…Behold, your God has not given you a few minted coins of gold, but He has endowed you with the mines themselves. He has not, as it were, handed you a cup of cold water, but He has brought you to the flowing fountain and given the well itself to you. God Himself is ours, 'The Lord is my portion, saith my soul.'" (Lamentations 3:24)

So today as you pray, give thanks for all your blessings. Your outlook will change, and you will see the positive things in your life that you never realized before.

# DAY 20

*Meeting God - Your Concerns Change*

> *"Seek first the kingdom of God and his righteousness,*
> *and all these things will be added to you."*
> Matthew 6:33

> *"Prayer does not change God,*
> *but it changes him who prays."*
> Søren Kierkegaard – Danish Philosopher & Theologian

In college, I loved to test the speed limits of my car. I never really thought of the dangers because I was young and full of ignorance. But when I got married and had children, speeding (and paying for tickets) did not seem so enticing any more. Why? My concerns changed. I was no longer concerned with a quick weekend thrill, but rather I was concerned about providing for my wife and children and being there for them.

This is what happens when we pray. Our concerns change. We begin with a large number of concerns, problems, worries, and anxieties. After being with Jesus for a while, praising Him and thanking Him, you have some new perspectives. You have fewer concerns, but still some remain. The question is, how do you deal with those? Jesus says,

"Come to me, all you who are weary and burdened, and I will give you rest. Take my yoke upon you and learn from me, for I am gentle and humble in heart, and you will find rest for your souls. For my yoke is easy and my burden is light." (Matthew 11:28-30)

Have you ever seen the guy at halftime of a sporting event who spins plates? He's good! He can keep at least 10 plates spinning at one time. Just as you think one of them is going to fall down he quickly gives it another spin and all is right again. We tend to think of ourselves like this guy, trying to keep all our problems spinning so they don't come crashing down on us. But the reality is, we can't. We were not created to, that is why we need to go to God in prayer.

He says to just forget the way you are trying to do this balancing act on your own, and to tell Him about all those worries that are on your plate. You talk to Him about all those problems, and things just sort of get rearranged. Things get balanced. And you are thinking that it just doesn't make any sense that those issues could be balanced – but He brings balance to your life and to your concerns. How does He do that?

## HOW DOES PRAYER HELP BALANCE?

The Bible says, "For the Lord gives wisdom, and from his mouth come knowledge and understanding. (Proverbs 2:6) God gives you wisdom to see your problems in a different way. "To the man who pleases him, God gives wisdom, knowledge and happiness..." (Ecclesiastes 2:26) He will balance your problems by giving you wisdom. He will also balance your problems by giving you strength. Isaiah 40:31 is a verse you need to memorize, "But those who hope in the Lord will renew their strength. They will soar on wings like eagles; they will run and not grow weary, they will walk and not be faint."

## A NEW FOCUS

Notice what this verse does NOT say, it does NOT say you won't have problems. Rather, it says God promises to give you strength amidst those problems. That strength comes from Jesus, and we receive it when we focus on Him. He says,

> "Remain in me, and I will remain in you. No branch can bear fruit by itself; it must remain on the vine. Neither can you bear fruit unless you remain in me. I am the vine; you are the branches. If a man remains in me and I in him, he will bear much fruit; apart from me you can do nothing." (John 15:4-5)

Did you notice how many times Jesus emphasizes "remain"? We have to be in Jesus; be in fellowship and walk with Him. When you think about your problems, your first consideration is to look at Jesus. "Remain in me," is a mandate that requires action. First you need to stay in daily, consistent prayer. As things and issues come outside your normal prayer time, you need to get into the habit of having impromptu conversations with God. Second, you need to stay in the Word. Methodically go through the Bible daily, learning to trust and obey. You need to surround yourself with Christian friends and counselors and to seek their support and encouragement.

The apostle Peter got a crash course on focus one day at sea. He was with the other disciples in a boat when they saw Jesus walking toward them. They were afraid and thought it was a ghost. Jesus said, "Take courage! It is I. Don't be afraid." (Matthew 14:27)

Then Peter gets this bright idea and says, "Lord, if it is you, tell me and I will come to you." And Jesus said, "Come." So Peter got out of the boat and started to walk on the water, but he saw the wind that was blowing and he was afraid. He took his eyes off Jesus, saw the problems around him and began to sink. He cried out, "Lord, help me!" And Jesus reached out and grabbed him. Our main concern now is to keep our eyes on Jesus. When you begin to look at the wind and waves around you, you begin to sink. But if you remain in Him and keep your eyes on Him, your life is going to balance and not fall apart.

"Turn your eyes upon Jesus, look full in His wonderful face, and the things of earth will grow strangely dim, in the light of His glory and grace."[1]

What are your concerns today? What are the plates that you are trying to balance right now? I encourage you to make a list of those and bring them to God, then be amazed at how He transforms your concern. So pray and be encouraged.

I hope today you gather the problems that are scattered throughout your life and you say, "Lord, these are my problems, I'm giving them to You. You balance them, and I'll keep my eyes on You."

---

1 "Turn Your Eyes Upon Jesus," Words and music by Helen H. Lemmel (1922).

# DAY 21

*"Be still, and know that I am God."*
Psalm 46:10

*"We have to pray with our eyes
on God, not on the difficulties."*
Oswald Chambers – Author, My Utmost for His Highest

I remember when my wife and I were expecting our first child (a girl). It was so exciting and nerve wracking as well. One of the things that I was nervous about – silly as it may sound – was what name to pick out. Now you'll have to know I am not the most creative person. So thinking of a name was hard for me.

Your name certainly does not define you, but it does have some meaning. My name (William) means, "conqueror" or "protection"[1] and that makes sense given the size of my giant biceps (or at least that's what I like to think). Throughout the Bible we see God changing people's names as their character changed. Jacob, whose name meant "deceiver,"

---

1   http://www.thinkbabynames.com/meaning/1/William

received the name Israel (God contended) after a wrestling match with God. Likewise, through the course of time there are many names given to God and each one carries with it a significant meaning. Today we're going to take a look at those and see how we can use them in prayer to help us understand God's identity.

## GOD'S NAMES

God is described throughout the Bible with names that illuminate His character, qualities and attributes. It might help when you pray if you talk to God each day about one of His Names and what it means to you. It will change your experience of meeting with Him.

Pick one today; the next day pick another one. You will find more and more of these as you read God's Word. Eventually, you will discover all of His Names. Here are a few to get you going.

- Elohim (Genesis 1:1), which simply means God. It is used 2,570 times in the Old Testament.
- El-Shaddai (Genesis 17:1), which means The Almighty God.
- Adonai (Malachi 1:6), which means Lord.
- Jehovah-Jireh (Genesis 22:13-14), which means the Lord will provide.
- Jehovah-Rapha, which means the Lord heals. (Exodus 15)
- Jehovah-Nissi, which means the Lord our banner. (Exodus 17)
- Jehovah-Maccaddeshem, which means the Lord sanctifies. (Leviticus 20)
- Jehovah-Shalom (Judges 6:24), which means God is our peace.
- Jehovah-Tsidkenu (Jeremiah 23:6), the Lord is our righteousness.
- Jehovah-Rohi (Psalm 23:1), the Lord is our Shepherd.
- Jehovah-Shammah (Ezekiel 48:35), which means the Lord is there.
- The Son of Righteousness. (Malachi 4:2)

Throughout the Bible He has many more names. Like the Lord of Hosts, the Commander of the Army of Angels. The Most High God. He is called The Mighty One. He is called The Branch, the Branch that gives us the sap of life. He is called The Holy One. He is called The

Judge. He is called The God of Seeing, He sees everything. He is called a jealous God. He is called Deliverer. He is called Savior, because He is the only One who can save us. He is called Redeemer. He is called Our Shield. He is called Strength. He is called The Righteous One. He is called The Everlasting God. He is called The God of Covenant, The Mighty God, God our Rock. He is called Wonderful Counselor, Mighty God, The Everlasting Father, The Prince of Peace, The Ancient of Days. He is called King; He is called Father; He is called The First and the Last.

## MORE NAMES

What about Jesus? Jesus' Name means Savior. He is called The Word; He is called Almighty; He is called Christ, which means Messiah, which means the Anointed One. The Holy Spirit also has different names – our Counselor, our Comforter, our Baptizer, our Advocate. He's called our Strengthener; our Sanctifier. He is called the Spirit of Christ; He is the seven fold Spirit of Revelations. He is the Spirit of Truth, the Spirit of Grace. He is the Spirit of Mercy, the Spirit of God, the Spirit of Holiness and the Spirit of Life.

## GOD'S ATTRIBUTES

What are some of the attributes of God? What is God like? You could talk to Him about this, too. God is Wisdom, (Romans 11:33) He is Infinity, meaning that God knows no boundaries, He is without any measure. He is Sovereign, that means He rules over His creation. He is Holiness, meaning God is set apart from every other creature in the universe because of His absolute perfect moral purity. He is the Trinity – God the Father; God the Son; God the Holy Spirit. He is Omniscient, which means He knows everything. He is Faithful, meaning everything that God has promised will come to pass. God is Love, not just an emotion or feeling, but a God of action. He is Omnipotent, which means He is all powerful. He is Omnipresent, which means He is everywhere at all times, at the same time. He is Self-existent; He said, "I Am who I Am. I Am the One who always Is." He is Self-sufficient, He doesn't need anything or anybody to keep Him going. He is also Justice, a just God. He is Immutable, which means He never changes. I talked to Him about that one today. He is Mercy, which means He is actively compassionate to His people. He is Eternal, which means He has no beginning and no end. He is Goodness, which means He wants to be kind and cordial and benevolent to mankind. He is Gracious, meaning He gives gifts to people who don't deserve it, because of His grace.

WOW! That's a lot. And just think, we can never exhaust what we say about God. In fact these names and these attributes only touch the surface of who God is. And yet, this is the God who invites us to pray to Him and who cares about us.

God's names and attributes should be acknowledged as you pray to Him. You might say, "Lord, today I want to talk to You about how You are my Banner, my Strength, my Song..." The good thing is, unlike me trying to pick a name for my daughter, we don't have to come up with something new. The Bible has already given us so many names that tell us so many things about God. Just take one of those attributes, one of those names, think on it, ruminate on it all day and see what God will do as you get to know Him better. This is how you can focus on God in prayer.

# week 4 | THE SCHOOL OF PRAYER

# DAY 22

*The School of Prayer – Professor Paul*

*"What you have learned and received and heard and seen in me – practice these things, and the God of peace will be with you."*
Philippians 4:9

*"It is in the light of Paul's practice , the way he lived, that we must interpret the statements he makes about his experience and behavior and about what we are to do."*
Dallas Willard – Theologian & Philosopher

When you go to school, you don't go to some empty room alone and attempt to teach everything to yourself. No, you go to a place where you can learn from people who really know the subject. We best learn from people smarter and more experienced. Think about it, even Tiger Woods, arguably the greatest golfer ever, goes to a swing coach. Tiger Woods goes to someone else to get help with his game. Just like a student, just like Tiger, we can best learn about prayer from the masters, the ones who have done it longest and best.

Today we're going to look at the beginning of The School of Prayer by looking at different "professors." You can learn a lot by listening to other people pray. You can learn a lot by what writers of Scripture have told us about how to pray. Today we'll be looking at "Professor Paul," and how to pray for other people.

Most of us pray shallow prayers, even for ourselves. We continually ask God to meet our immediate needs. Today we're going to look at how to pray with substance, but where do we start? First, look at what Paul says, "For this reason I kneel before the Father..." (Ephesians 3:14)

## USING THE POWER OF THE HOLY SPIRIT

Typically, Jews would stand to pray, but Paul said he was so humbled going into God's presence that he was going to kneel. In verse 16 he goes on to say, "I pray that out of his glorious riches he may strengthen you with power through his Spirit in your inner being..."

"Out of His glorious riches," how much does God have? He has everything. There is no limit to what God can give spiritually or physically. "He may strengthen you with power," what kind of power? The kind of power that raised Jesus from the dead is at God's disposal. He can give you that kind of power in your inner being. This power can fill you with encouragement, which Paul had talked about a few verses earlier. Paul said he wanted the people to be just the opposite of being discouraged and downcast; he wanted them to be indomitable (never weakened) in their spirit. That's the kind of power God can give you and wants to give you. Paul prayed this for believers in Ephesus, that they would have that indomitable spirit. How do you get that? Through the Holy Spirit. We receive the Holy Spirit the moment we put our faith in Jesus. He comes to live inside us. Paul prayed that through the Holy Spirit, the people would be unstoppable.

Did you see the Captain America movie that came out in the summer of 2011, or do you at least know the story? Steve Rogers is physically pathetic. He's about 5'6", 110 pounds, but he has an unconquerable spirit; the spirit of Superman. We are like Steve Rogers, initially, pretty lame on the outside. But when we become Christians, God fills us with His Spirit and great power. The analogy goes on. Because of Rogers' great spirit, he is chosen for a super secret program that changes his body to match his spirit. He comes out massive, super strong and super fast; the perfect soldier. Likewise, as the Spirit works in us, we become more and more like God. Our lives and actions begin to match our spirit. God makes us into the perfect spiritual soldiers. Maybe our bodies are not so super. But inside, we are powerful. You might hear some discouraging news today, the person you want to win the presidency is falling behind, or a problem with your spouse defies solution. But it's okay. God is in control, and you can receive this indomitable spirit through the Holy Spirit.

## FOR INHABITABLE HEARTS

Paul prays for a second thing, "So that Christ may dwell in your hearts through faith…" (Ephesians 3:17) He prayed that Christ would be "at home" in us, that He would feel welcome in our lives and in our hearts. And when He dwells in us, guess what happens? Our thoughts, attitudes and emotions change. How does this happen? "Through faith." He dwells in us. Christ will be comfortable in us if we are trusting in Him.

There is a humorous story about a little girl who is confused about the whole idea of Jesus living inside of her heart. Perplexed, she asks her mommy, "Mom, if Jesus is living inside of me, wouldn't he be sticking out everywhere?" Yes, exactly! He should be sticking out everywhere! The young girl's limited perspective had her thinking in only physical terms, but she is exactly right. Jesus is so great, so big spiritually, that if He is truly inside us, it will be impossible for Him not to "stick out," to overflow into every aspect of our lives.

If you are trusting in your money, your job, your relationships, or other people – do you think Jesus will be comfortable making Himself at home with you? Can you pray with depth if Jesus is not dwelling in you?

## FOR AN UNDERSTANDING OF CHRIST'S LOVE

Paul continues, "…And I pray that you, being rooted and established in love, may have power, together with all the saints, to grasp how wide and long and high and deep is the love of Christ…" (Ephesians 3:17-18) Paul is saying he wants his readers to understand – wants us to understand – Christ's love for us. I'm convinced that we would never be the same if we understood just how much Jesus loves us. It will change you forever to understand how wide Christ's love is – it's as wide as the world. How deep it is – deeper than the depths of despair, discouragement and even death. How long Christ's love is – as long as your life, as long as eternity. How high Christ's love is – as high as the highest emotion. Christ's love is immense, beyond our understanding.

When you pray knowing the magnitude of God's love, you have immeasurable faith that God can accomplish the unimaginable.

## FOR AN EXPERIENCE OF GOD'S LOVE

Fourth, Paul prays "…and to know this love that surpasses knowledge – that you may be filled to the measure of all the fullness of God." (Ephesians 3:19) Paul prays that you would not just know, but *experience* God's love, thereby becoming full of God. Do not just quickly pass over that phrase, "all the fullness of God." What an amazing promise that we will be so filled. God promises us His own fullness. Perfection is the goal. Though we will obviously never be God, He promises to make us more and more like Him, the ultimate ideal. Our only access to such blessing is through prayer. Oswald Chambers writes, "Prayer is the exercise of drawing on the grace of God." If we don't acknowledge His limitless grace, we neglect the full impact of this blessing. So understanding how God's grace unleashes powerful blessings goes to the real need in the lives of these believers.

Oswald Chambers can again help us here. He writes, "Our common ideas regarding prayer are not found in the New Testament. We look upon prayer simply as a means of getting things for ourselves, but the biblical purpose of prayer is that we may get to know God Himself." He goes on, "Prayer is not a matter of changing things externally, but one of working miracles in a person's inner nature."[1] Our prayer must first be about God and our relationship with Him. The other stuff is second to this. "Seek first the kingdom of God and his righteousness, and all these things will be added to you" (Matthew 6:33).

Paul ends this prayer, "Now to him who is able to do immeasurably more than all we ask or imagine." (Ephesians 3:20) God can do more than we can ask or even imagine – think of that. That's the kind of God you serve. Paul writes, "In the same way, the Spirit helps us in our weakness. We do not know what we ought to pray for, but the Spirit himself intercedes for us with groans that words cannot express." (Romans 8:26) Even when we don't know what to pray, the Spirit is right there asking for us. What an encouragement! When you pray for other people, pray for what they really need, a walk with Christ that changes everything. That is a real prayer. Professor Paul, you have taught us well.

When you pray for people, what kind of prayers do you pray? Are you praying that they will be strengthened with His Holy Spirit? That they would understand God's love? That they would feel God's grace? Look at your prayer life as it pertains to other people and think about how deep it is.

---

1  Oswald Chambers. My Utmost for His Highest. Grand Rapids: Discovery House Publishing, 1992. August 28.

# DAY 23

*The School of Prayer – Professor Jesus*
*The Lord's Prayer*

*"He was despised and rejected by men; a man of sorrows, and acquainted with grief; and as one from whom men hid their faces he was despised, and we esteemed him not."*
Isaiah 53:3 ESV

*"Jesus wants to teach us that praying, to be a genuine act of righteousness, must be without ostentation, directed to the Father and not to men, primarily private, and devoid of the delusion that God can be manipulated by empty garrulity."*
D.A. Carson – Trinity Evangelical Divinity School

If you really wanted to learn basketball, wouldn't Michael Jordan, arguably the greatest of all time, be the best teacher? If the option is available to learn from the best, why choose anyone else? Maybe we'll never have the opportunity to learn basketball from Michael Jordan, but we do have a much greater opportunity available to us every day. We can learn how to pray from the Master Himself, Jesus.

We're going to look at The Lord's Prayer for the next couple of days. The Lord's Prayer is really a prayer that Jesus told the disciples to pray. But for centuries it has been called The Lord's Prayer, and I'm not going to attempt to rename it here. The disciples went to Jesus and said, "Lord, teach us how to pray." This is important. Note that Jesus gives the Lord's Prayer in direct response to the question of how the disciples were to pray. When Jesus says you should pray like this, we should pay attention. He had preached sermons that were amazing and had performed astounding miracles. Yet the disciples said they wanted to pray like He prayed. They had seen Him praying, and they were amazed at that. Jesus knew how to pray.

## THE MODEL

The Lord's Prayer is a pattern for prayer. It's not really something to be repeated over and over and over again. It's a model. J.I. Packer writes, "Did Jesus intend that they should repeat the words, parrot fashion? No. This prayer is a pattern for all Christian praying. Jesus is teaching that prayer will be acceptable when, and only when, the attitudes, thoughts, and desires expressed fit the pattern. That is to say, every prayer of ours should be fashioned after the Lord's Prayer in some shape or form."[1] So let's take a look at it.

## RESPECT & INTIMACY

There are actually six requests in The Lord's Prayer – three that involve the glory of God and three that involve man's wellbeing. Similar to the Ten Commandments, there are four commandments that involve God's glory and six that involve mankind. He starts with "Our Father." Jesus always prayed to the Father. There is never an example of Him praying any other way. But you will not find one person in the Old Testament praying to "Our Father." Although the Fatherhood of God is taught in the Old Testament, He was never prayed to in that way. So this was a revolutionary thought for the average Jew. And when Jesus used the word "Father," He used the word Abba that we would call "Daddy," a name a child would call his father, not the formal form of father. We are God's children.

The Bible says, "Yet to all who received him, to those who believed in

---

1    J.I. Packer. *Praying the Lord's Prayer*. Wheaton: Crossway, 2007. 15-16.

his name, he gave the right to become *children* of God. (John 1:12) As the children of God, we should call Him "Father." Your kids hopefully don't go around calling you Jim or Bob or whatever your first name is. No, it's a sign of both *respect and intimacy* for them to call you Father or Daddy.

"Because you are sons, God sent the Spirit of his Son into our hearts, the Spirit who calls out, 'Abba, Father.'" (Galatians 4:6)

## RULER OF EVERYTHING

So, we pray "Father in heaven." Jesus says, "in heaven." This gets us away from that flippancy that sometimes people get when they talk to God in prayer and regard Him almost as a celestial teddy bear. He is holy; He is sovereign, that means He rules over everything; He is our Father, but He is "in heaven" ruling. We do not pray like Ricky Bobby in Talladega Nights who imagines God in whatever way makes him feel most comfortable when he says, "I like the Christmas Jesus best, and I'm saying grace! When you say grace, you can say it to grown-up Jesus, teenage Jesus, bearded Jesus, or whomever you want." We pray with reverence and in awe of who He is. He is also, "our Father" – not just Jesus' Father, but our Father as well. Because Jesus starts with "Our Father in heaven," we can approach God's throne with confidence, since He is in charge of everything.

There was a missionary who was teaching a Hindu woman how to pray, and she started with this prayer, "Our Father in heaven." And the Hindu woman said, "Stop. That's enough. That's all I needed to hear. There is no need to fear anymore. He's our Father." So we can approach Him confidently. We can also approach Him with simplicity, like a child would; we can approach Him with love.

## REMEMBER TO GLORIFY

Next, there are three requests that come to glorify God. The three requests are for Your Name, Your kingdom and Your will. First, look at the word "Hallowed." To hallow simply means to make holy, or sacred, or to consecrate. God's Name is to be hallowed, worshipped. We reviewed this before when we were considering the names of God in chapter 21. That is one way we can do it. Another way we can hallow God's Name is to not profane it by using profane language, telling dirty stories, or just not worshipping His Name. Understanding God is also important if we are going to hallow His Name. We need to know who He is.

"Your kingdom come," Jesus says. That means we are going to pray that God's program for the world will be fulfilled. We are praying for the return of Jesus, and we are told to pray this every single day. This is God's will for us. When you do that, it gets you re-calibrated as to what God's program really is; what we ought to be striving for. Our little plans and little schemes are not so important anymore.

## PRESCRIPTIVE "WILL"

Last, we are to pray for "His will to be done on earth as it is in heaven," which means "perfectly." That means we are going to pray that God's will is going to become our will; that we want what He wants. Just a few verses later, Jesus tells us to "seek first the kingdom of God" and then He will take care of everything else (Matthew 5:33). If our will is aligned with God's will, He will support and provide for us. The Bible says that whenever we pray that way, we receive according to the will of God. We are also praying that God's will might prevail over the entire earth. Some might ask, "If God is sovereign, why isn't His will always done perfectly?" We sometimes get confused when talking about God's will because the term is used as a catch-all to describe different things. It is generally used in two ways, usually called God's decretive and prescriptive will. God's decretive will refers to God's eternal plans and decrees; it is His sovereign rule over everything. This will cannot be thwarted and is always done over all the earth (Daniel 4:35). God's prescriptive will is different. It refers to God's desire, what God commands and wants man to do. This will clearly can be thwarted, since all of us using the will He's given us constantly disobey what God has commanded. So, God's decretive will is how things are, and His prescriptive will is how things ought to be. This is the cause of confusion over God's will not being done over the whole. His decretive will is absolutely always done. God is sovereign and in control over situations that even include sin and evil. However His prescriptive will is not always done. We know that His will doesn't get done perfectly because the Bible says He doesn't want "...anyone to perish, but everyone to come to repentance." (2 Peter 3:9) And we know that doesn't happen. So we are going to ask God that His will be done on earth as it is in heaven – and that gets us to thinking about getting our will in line with His will.

So in prayer, we begin by focusing on God and not ourselves. We pray for His name to be hallowed, for His kingdom to come, and for His will to be done. John Stott, a theologian, writes:

> "Prayer is not a convenient device for imposing our will upon God, or bending his will to ours, but the prescribed way of subordinating our will to his. It is by prayer that we seek God's will, embrace it and align ourselves with it. Every true prayer is a variation on the theme, 'Your will be done.' Our Master taught us to say this in the pattern prayer He gave us and added the supreme example of it in Gethsemane."

Prayer is first about God and what He wants, then about us and what we want.

# DAY 24

*The School of Prayer – Professor Jesus*
*The Lord's Prayer*

*"After he had dismissed them, he went up*
*into the hills by himself to pray."*
Matthew 14:23

*"The disciples were to learn about prayer, not simply by repeating*
*the model prayer Jesus provided, but by observing the example of*
*Jesus as He consistently went off by Himself to pray."*
*Alistair Begg – Senior Pastor Parkside*

I remember as a student at Master's Seminary, there was one professor that every student wanted. No, it wasn't because he was the easiest; it was because he had an unmatched ability to teach in a way that made things stick. Students flocked to his classes because they knew that they were learning from the best. When it comes to prayer, Jesus is that professor. So let's take another look at the Lord's Prayer and see what else Jesus has to say about prayer.

We are with Professor Jesus, looking at The Lord's Prayer. Today we are going to look at the second half of that prayer and see what kinds of requests we can make for ourselves. There are really three parts to this: give us, forgive us, and lead us. Jesus prays, "Give us today our daily bread." (Matthew 6:11)

## WHY IS "DAILY" A KEY?

All the requests in this prayer are daily requests. The key word here is "daily." We are daily asking that our focus be on the return of Jesus; daily hallowing God's Name; daily needing forgiveness; daily needing God to lead us, and we are daily needing God to provide for our needs. So often we ask God for things that will make us never need Him again. Instead we should pray as a writer in Proverbs does, "…give me neither poverty nor riches; feed me with the food that is needful for me, lest I be full and deny you and say, 'Who is the Lord?' Or lest I be poor and steal." (Proverbs 30:8-9) We often pray, "Lord, please give me a million dollars; Lord, please let this business deal go through." We are in effect saying, "Lord, I don't want to have to trust You as much as I trust You right now. I'm having to trust You every day just to get my needs met." And God says, "Exactly." And that's how it's supposed to be. Truly, even people who have lots of money still have to focus on God on a daily basis. For example, no one can guarantee his own health. Only God can do that.

## KEEP MY PRIDE IN CHECK

Physical needs are what we are dealing with when we talk about "daily bread." Not just food; it can be the house payment, your health, anything you need God to help you with on a daily basis. God truly is the source of all blessings. "Every good and perfect gift is from above, coming down from the Father of the heavenly lights, who does not change like shifting shadows." (James 1:17)

Isn't it amazing that our Creator is the One we are looking to for our next bread, our next mortgage payment and for our eternal destiny? We are completely reliant upon Him. And who better to rely on than the One who, before the world began, knew what you would need. As He was creating the world, He did it in such a way that before man was created, He put plants here so there would be something to eat; full-grown trees with fruit so that we could survive. He was providing for our needs even before we were present. As we pray for our daily needs to be met, this prevents us from thinking that we have pulled ourselves up by our own bootstraps. We did not make it happen all by ourselves! We get the idea, "I worked, I got a paycheck, I paid the bills." Where did the job come from? Who gave you the ability to work? Who gave you the reasoning capacity needed to do the job? All of that comes from the Creator. It's like the kid who boasts about the one dollar a week he gets from doing his chores. His parents provide the chores, the house in which he lives where he can do the chores, and the compensation for the chores. In fact, he owes his physical life to them. They produced him! It would be ridiculous for this kid to feel pride about anything, especially making his measly one dollar. How much more ridiculous then is it for us to take pride in anything we do since we are even more helpless than the kid, and God provides for us infinitely more than the parent does for the child?

## FORGIVING SINS

The second thing prayed for is "forgive us our debts as we forgive our debtors." We are asking for the forgiveness of sins. Sin is the ultimate separator between mankind and God. It is what prevents us from fellowshipping with God or getting into His presence. Holy God cannot have fellowship with sinful human beings. You might ask, "Why are we asking God each day to forgive our sins? I thought God did that when I got saved." The answer is that He did give you judicial forgiveness for your sins at the moment you asked Him into your life. When He became the Lord of your life, all of your sins were wiped out before God. You no longer have to answer for those sins. However, practically, you still sin. I know you and I know me, and I know what the Bible says about us. We still sin. "If we say we have no sin, we deceive ourselves, and the truth is not in us." (1 John 1:8)

So what needs to happen? Daily we need to ask for forgiveness for our sins. This is not a prayer repeated by rote, "Lord, just forgive us our debt as we forgive our debtors." That doesn't quite cut it, and that's why this prayer is only a model. It helps us to say instead of "forgive us our debts," to say, "Lord, forgive me for going 45 back there in a 25 mile an hour zone. Lord, forgive me for how I snapped at one of the kids today; that was wrong. Lord, forgive me for not getting up and spending time with You like I should; I'm sorry I hit that snooze button." You specifically confess your sins to God. "If we confess our sins, he is faithful and just and will forgive us our sins and purify us from all unrighteousness." (1 John 1:9)

If we don't confess our sins, we don't get forgiveness of our sins. And there is one other problem here. If you don't forgive other people their sins against you, you also do not get forgiveness. Jesus says, "For if you forgive men when they sin against you, your heavenly Father will also forgive you. But if you do not forgive men their sins, your Father will not forgive your sins." (Matthew 6:14 & 15)

If you have bitterness in your heart for other believers, and are unwilling to forgive them for whatever reason, God doesn't forgive your sins either. If one of your kids punches the other kid and then genuinely repents and apologizes, but the punched kid refuses to forgive, he is in effect punching the first kid back and sinning himself. You do not let this kid off the hook until he deals with his anger and forgives his brother. Likewise, when there is sin between you and God, your prayers are not going to get answered. We are going to be dealing more with this later.

Jesus puts it this way in Matthew 18, "Therefore, the kingdom of heaven is like a king who wanted to settle accounts with his servants." So the king has one servant who owes 10,000 talents, more than could ever be repaid in his lifetime. A talent was equal to about 6,000 drachmas, which was equivalent to about 20 years worth of work for the average person. In modern equivalents, say that the average worker made

$15 an hour. At 2,000 hours per year he would make $30,000. So a talent would equal $600,000. Thus 10,000 talents, in today's terms, would be about $6 billion, a ridiculously large debt that none of us could ever dream of paying.[1] So the king says to him, "Okay, we'll sell your wife and your children into slavery and get the debt paid off that way." The man got down on his hands and knees and begged the king for pity. The king relented and granted forgiveness of the debt. The debtor was pretty happy about that, so happy that he went out and found one of his own servants and demanded a meager loan repayment. The other servant got down on his hands and knees and begged for more time to repay the loan. But he was told, "No way," and he was beaten and sent to prison until he could repay the debt. It is estimated that Bernie Madoff stole about $13 billion from investors. This would be like a judge deciding to cancel Madoff's debt and to free him from prison, and then Madoff going straight to one of his friends and demanding that he repay him $10. Ridiculous! $13 billion compared to 10 measly dollars. Well, the other servants heard about this and they went to the king who had forgiven the big debt. Jesus said this, "Then the master called the servant in. 'You wicked servant,' he said, 'I canceled all that debt of yours because you begged me to. Shouldn't you have had mercy on your fellow servant just as I had on you?' In anger, his master turned him over to the jailers to be tortured, until he should pay back all he owed. This is how my heavenly Father will treat each of you unless you forgive your brother from your heart." (Matthew 18:35) We have got to forgive others their sin against us if we expect our sin to be forgiven by God.

# FIND THE ESCAPE HATCH

Lastly, Jesus says, "Lead us not into temptation…" (Matthew 6:13) Now we know God doesn't tempt us. James says, "When tempted, no one should say, 'God is tempting me.' For God cannot be tempted by evil, nor does he tempt anyone…" (James 1:13)

---

1   ESV Study Bible, note on Matthew 18:24, p. 1859.

Paul goes even further and says,

> "No temptation has seized you except what is common to man. And God is faithful; he will not let you be tempted beyond what you can bear. But when you are tempted, he will also provide a way out so that you can stand up under it." (1 Corinthians 10:13)

God won't let you get "over tempted," and actually provides an "escape hatch" for every tempting situation. What you pray for is, "Lord, You know what I am being tempted with today. Help me find the escape hatch. Let me escape this temptation. Give me a way out."

In summary, our prayers should be mindful of Jesus' instructions. We should acknowledge that our needs are daily; we need to forgive and be forgiven of our sins; and, lastly, we need to know we live in a world full of temptation. But there is always an escape hatch provided. So, pray to the Lord and ask Him to give, forgive and lead.

# DAY 25

*The School of Prayer – Professor Jabez*

"Behold, the LORD'S hand is not so short that it cannot
save; Nor is his ear so dull that it cannot hear."
Isaiah 59:1

"Jabez doesn't stand astride the Old Testament like a
Moses or a David or light up the book of Acts like those
early Christians who turned the world upside down.
But one thing is sure: The little difference in his life
made all the difference."
Bruce Wilkinson – Author, Prayer of Jabez

I remember as a kid hanging out with my dad while he did his Saturday afternoon chores. He owned a car wash so he would have to fix broken equipment, clean out dirty bays, and count quarters. As a five year-old I thought there was nothing my dad couldn't do. In my eyes he was all powerful! Hopefully this is something that you are realizing about God. Of course, as I grew up I realized that my dad was not all powerful like God. One of the greatest ways we see and experience God's awesome power is through the blessings that he pours out in our lives. Today we're going to look at a unique prayer of blessing in the Bible, it's a prayer that not only teaches us about God's ability to bless, but also why it is that God blesses.

1 Chronicles chapter 4 contains a list of names punctuated by

the mention of Jabez in verse 9. The one thing that made Jabez stand out from the crowd around him was his prayer. It wasn't his brains, strength, or an idea; it was his prayer that he prayed to God asking to be blessed. God answered it.

## PRAYER FOR PERSONAL BLESSING

Before we look at Jabez's prayer I need to add something. Jabez and his prayer have been criticized to both extremes by many commentators. Some have said that his prayer is selfish. How dare we ask God for a blessing for ourselves? I disagree. Expressing our needs to God in prayer is an act of faith, not selfishness. Others have overstated this prayer by asserting that if it is used properly, it guarantees your request. As stated previously, God only gives us gifts that we need, not ones that would harm us. So, there is no guarantee that God will answer our prayers in the manner in which we expect. We are told over and over in the Bible that "we have not because we ask not." (James 4:2) That being said, let's look at Jabez.

## FAITH WINS

The odds were stacked against Jabez. The Bible says, "Jabez was more honorable than his brothers. His mother had named him Jabez, saying, "I gave birth to him in pain." (1 Chronicles 4:9) The name Jabez was the Hebrew word for pain. He started off with a name that was far from positive. Names in those days said a lot about how your parents felt about you, and how other people would feel about you. It would basically be like naming your son Cancer; not a good start for the child.

Maybe you feel that you were born with the odds stacked against you. A dysfunctional family, divorced parents, abuse, and so on, the odds were against you. Some feel their lives started well and have become bad. You've lost your job, maybe your spouse has just left you. Maybe your health is bad or you deal with constant pain. What are the odds of God intervening for you? At your age, what are the odds of God using you for an extraordinary task? It's about a little faith in a great God. God is Sovereign. After all, what were the odds of the Red Sea parting in front of the Israelites, allowing them to walk through on dry land?

## THE FIRST REQUEST

Jabez prayed, "Oh, that you would bless me..." (1 Chronicles 4:10) Is it okay to ask God to bless me? Absolutely! From where else do blessings come? "Every good and perfect gift is from above, coming down from the Father of the heavenly lights, who does not change like shifting shadows." (James 1:17) If you don't ask God to be blessed, you just get what you do ask for. Ask Him. There is only one prayer in the Bible that doesn't have a request of God. It's the one prayer that Jesus condemned – the prayer of the Pharisee who goes to the mountain top and says, "Oh, Lord, I thank You that I'm not like this guy over here." And Jesus says, "Do you think he came down off that mountain forgiven? Think again." We need to ask God for a blessing. You can ask Him for a general blessing, "Lord, just bless me today." Or you can ask Him for something specific. I do both. Why not?

## THE SECOND REQUEST

Jabez prayed, "...and enlarge my territory!" He is asking that he would have greater influence for God. God often increases the influence of faithful people. Daniel became one of the presidents in Babylon. Joseph was promoted to second in charge in Egypt. Abraham was given more flocks, more herds, and more servants, which came with more territory. The apostle Paul saw influence grow to touch the known world before his death. It is a great prayer to say, "Lord, increase my influence for You."

## THE THIRD REQUEST

Jabez prayed, "Let your hand be with me..." If you have accepted

Jesus, God's presence is always with you. He is omnipresent; everywhere at the same time. However, we tend to forget this huge truth! So we can say, "Lord, help me to remember that You are with me and to listen for Your voice." Jesus said in John 10:27 that His sheep would know His voice and follow Him. God can direct you when you are listening to His voice. The Bible says "The steps of a good man are ordered by the Lord." (Psalm 37:23) So ask Him to order your steps.

## THE FOURTH REQUEST

Lastly, Jabez prays, "...and keep me from harm so that I will be free from pain." Nothing will cause us pain like living in sin. Take this opportunity to ask God to keep us out of sinful situations that will harm us. Pray, "Lord, please deliver me from temptation." The Bible says, "The Lord knows how to rescue godly men from temptations…" (2 Peter 2:9) You know the temptations that have caused you to fall in the past. Pray for deliverance from those specific temptations. Then ask God to deliver you from those temptations you don't even know about. This will keep you out of a lot of trouble and pain.

This prayer, while not a magic formula, is life-changing. I challenge you to pray it. "Lord, that You would bless me; Lord, that You would enlarge my territory; that You would go with me and keep me from sin and harm."

# DAY 26

*The School of Prayer – Professor Jacob*

*"The Lord said...I am with you and will
watch over you wherever you go, and I
will bring you back to this land, I will not leave
you until I have done what I have promised you."*
*Genesis 28:15*

*"The great fault of the children of God is, they do not
continue in prayer; they do not go on praying; they do
not persevere. If they desire anything for God's glory, they
should pray until they get it."*
*George Muller – Director of Orphan Houses 1800s*

We are addicted to stories of perseverance in the midst of difficulty. We love the little guy who just won't quit. From Rudy[1], to Frodo[2], to the Little Engine That Could, we want to root for the hardworking underdog and see him succeed. We respect and encourage perseverance, and so does God, particularly when it comes to prayer.

Today we're going to look at "Professor Jacob" and at what he can teach us about prayer. Jacob teaches us to not give up; to never relent in prayer. We pick up Jacob's prayer as he is getting ready to meet with his

---

1   From the motion picture "Rudy" depicting the struggles and success of Daniel "Rudy" Ruettiger. Rudy was a 5' 6" football player who dreamed of playing for Notre Dame.

2   Frodo Baggins is a fictional character in J. R. R. Tolkien's Lord of the Rings trilogy. Frodo undertakes an impossible task of destroying Bilbo's magic ring.

brother, Esau. He had deceived Esau a couple of times and they hadn't seen each other for 20 years. Jacob was afraid this might be their last meeting because Easu might want to kill him. So, Jacob prays and asks God for strength and survival. During this midnight prayer time Jacob is met by an angel, whom he wrestles with for a blessing. "When the man (the angel) saw that he could not overpower him, he touched the socket of Jacob's hip so that his hip was wrenched as he wrestled with the man. Then the man said, 'Let me go, for it is daybreak.' But Jacob replied, 'I will not let you go unless you bless me.'" (Genesis 32:25-26)

Now this wasn't just any angel. This was the angel of the Lord, which is a pre-incarnate appearance of Jesus Christ. Jacob is literally wrestling with Jesus in prayer and said he was not going to let go until he had received a blessing. "Then the man asked him, 'What is your name?' 'Jacob,' he answered. Then the man said, 'Your name will no longer be Jacob, but Israel, because you have struggled with God and with men and have overcome.'" (Genesis 32:27-28)

## BE PERSISTENT

From this passage we learn that we don't just give up when we pray for something once and say, "Well, I did pray and it didn't happen, so I guess I'm done." No, we're not interested in people who give up easily, and neither is God. We don't watch movies about people who try something once and then quit. We are naturally drawn to stories of persistence. God implanted that within you. God is like that too. You ask and you ask and you ask again. And when you do that, one of the things that happens is your character changes. As you struggle with God in prayer, your character changes, just as Jacob's did. His name was Jacob, which meant "deceiver," and it was a pretty accurate description of his character. But after this event, his name became Israel, which meant "prince with God," and his character was different. No longer was he a deceiver; now he was a person of God. And when you go to God in prayer and you continually ask, you are going to find that you will begin to change inside.

# JESUS CONFIRMS

Jesus highlights the power of persistence through a story. He tells about a man in bed with his family at midnight. They are awakened by a knock at the door. It's a friend who says, "Hey, I need three loaves of bread. A buddy of mine just unexpectedly arrived in town and my cupboard is bare." So the home owner says, "That's your problem, my kids are asleep, the door is locked. Go home!" But the friend keeps knocking! So, finally the man gets up and gives him bread because he doesn't want this guy waking up his whole family. Then Jesus told them the point of the story. He says, keep asking, keep seeking, keep knocking. That's what God wants you to do.

# THE FEARLESS JUDGE

Then Jesus told His disciples a parable. Why? "To show them that they should always pray and not give up." (Luke 18:1) We give up too easily! The parable begins, "In a certain town there was a judge who neither feared God nor cared about men." (Luke 18:2) This judge doesn't care about God, so justice is out the window. And he doesn't care about people, so mercy is out the window. This is a very dangerous person, and he is a judge! So what happens? "Now there was a widow in that town who kept coming to him with the plea, 'Grant me justice against my adversary.'" (Luke 18:3) Now who could mean less to him than a widow? Nobody. She can't file suit against him; she is just a widow with nothing. But she does have one thing…persistence. "For some time he refused. But finally he said to himself, 'Even though I don't fear God or care about men, yet because this widow keeps bothering me, I will see that she gets justice, so that she won't eventually wear me out with her coming!'" (Luke 18:5-6)

The judge in this story is a horrible, unjust person. He doesn't represent God in this parable. He represents the antithesis of God and yet he finally gives in to the widow's persistence. "Listen to what the unjust judge says. He will only keep putting them off for so long" (Luke 18:6) Jesus is saying, if a bad judge gives someone something because they are persistent, how much more will we receive from God, since He loves us.

God wants to give you what you need. But why would He ask us to wait? Puritan Pastor Thomas Watson tackled the question, "Why would God ever keep us asking and seeking and knocking when he could respond sooner?" He gives four answers:

1. Because He loves to hear the voice of prayer. "You let the musician play a great while before you throw him down money, because you love to hear this music."

2. That He may humble us. We may too easily assume we merit some ready answer, or that He is at our beck and call like a butler; not as sovereign Lord and loving Father.

3. Because He sees we are not yet fit or ready for the mercy we seek. It may be He has things to put in place – in us or in our church or in the world. There are a million pieces to the puzzle. Some things go first to make a place for the others.

4. Finally, that the mercy we pray for may be the more prized, and may be sweeter when it comes.

Today, here's the question: Are you willing to persevere to unleash God's power? Do you have the intestinal fortitude to say, "I am not going to stop until this happens. I know that if it is Your will for it to happen, then I'm going to trust You for it, and I'm going to continue to ask and ask, in faith, that You are going to do it." If you're ready for God to meet your needs, then I hope today you will ask Him for something persistently. And in the process, your character will be changed.

# DAY 27

*The School of Prayer – Praying with Others*

*"For where two or three are gathered
in my name, there am I among them."*
Matthew 18:20

*"Praying regularly with others can be one of the
most enriching adventures of your Christian life.
Most of the great movements of God can be traced to
a small group of people he called together to begin praying."*
Donald Whitney – Southern Baptist Theological Seminary

Most experts agree that we all learn through three different methods – reading, writing and listening. The same goes for prayer. While reading and writing are extremely important, listening can be a catalyst to build faith and confidence when we pray. Let me explain.

## MODELS OF CORPORATE PRAYER

One of the ways you can learn to pray better is by praying with other believers. This is a biblical concept. Throughout Scripture you find believers praying together. In the upper room, 120 believers were huddled together praying for the Holy Spirit to come as Jesus had promised. When Peter was in prison, there was a prayer meeting going on where they were asking God to release him. Before Jesus was going to the cross, He went to Gethsemane to pray with other believers. Why does the Lord want us to pray together? For many reasons. Do you remember learning to drive a stick shift? You wonder if you will ever figure it out. Then you watch someone else drive that car and you just know that you can do it, too. Praying together lets you see the process you can apply to your own prayer life.

## EXCITEMENT FOR GOD RUBS OFF

One of the things you get when you pray with others is fervency. When you see others fervently asking God for things, it tells you how to pray. It also helps you to grab onto faith. When you see other believers praying in faith and hear how God answers their prayers, your faith grows. It also gives you a great sense of family. Charles Finney, a 19th Century evangelist, once said, "Nothing tends more to cement the hearts of Christians than praying together. Never do they love one another so well as when they witness the outpouring of each other's hearts in prayer."[1] Just today I got to pray with a brother in Christ and encourage him. It was a reminder that we are all a part of the same family of God. It's such an encouragement to know someone else is praying for me and over me. It also gives a sense of familiarity with other Christians. This is probably seen best in marriage. When you pray with your spouse, it helps you to know their heart; to know how each of you is doing spiritually. If you don't believe me, try praying together after a serious disagreement – it often compels you to make up. It also gives you a great habit for the rest of your life.

## ELIMINATE THE DISTRACTIONS

One distraction of praying together with other Christians is that our minds just wander. Maybe you've been in a situation with 20 other

---

1   Charles G. Finney. Lectures on Revivals of Religions. Chapter VIII.

people and you are all going to pray, one by one – and you are number 15! Or you begin to worry that all of your thoughts have already been prayed about. You know you have some time before your number is up and you are thinking about what is for lunch, thinking about what tomorrow will bring – then you feel a little guilty about that. What can you do when people are praying and it isn't your turn? Here are some suggestions.

## TOPICAL PRAYERS

Number one, pray by topic. If someone brings up Suzie Lou and they are praying for Suzie to be saved, pray by topic. When they are praying, you talk to God about Suzie, too, let that be the topic. Then you are always praying for the same thing. You can also pray by using Scripture. Maybe someone else is praying for another to be saved – think of Scriptures that apply so that when you go to the Lord in prayer, you can refer to that Scripture. Perhaps saying, "Lord, I know it is Your will that this person be saved because You say in Scripture that it is not Your will that any should perish." If the prayer is to deliver someone from alcohol or drug abuse, think of a Scripture that backs that up. Another method of group prayer is to pray aloud at the same time. Culturally, this doesn't work for a lot of people, but you might want to try it if your mind tends to wander off during prayer. You might even overhear the prayer of another and pray the same thing.

## POPCORN PRAYER

Another suggestion is "popcorn prayers." What that means is you might be in a group of 20, but no one prays a long prayer. The prayers are more sentence prayers and it can go all over the room with no order as to who prays next. Charles Spurgeon, a great pastor, used to say, "True prayer is measured by weight, not by length. A single groan before God may have more fullness of prayer in it than a fine oration of great length." The prayers just go up to God in a "popcorn" fashion.

When you put those kernels of corn into a hot pan, you really don't know which one will pop first – and it doesn't matter.

## SMALLER GROUPS

Lastly, if you are in a large group, you could break up into smaller groups to pray. This will help eliminate the problem of waiting for your turn. In a smaller group, your turn comes up more quickly.

When praying with others, the most important thing to remember is who else is praying with you. S. D. Gordon writes, "If there are two persons praying, there are three. If three meet to pray, there are four praying. There is always one more than you can see."[2] The Holy Spirit is always praying with us and that is where our power, where our effectiveness comes from.

When it comes to praying with others, the bottom line is that more is caught than taught. You will learn to pray by listening to other believers pray. Have you been praying with your children? Have you been praying with your wife? What about Christian friends? Make today the first day of a new life of prayer with your family and other believers around you.

2 S.D. Gordon, *Quiet Talks on Prayer* (New York: Fleming H. Revell Co., 1904), 130.

# DAY 28

*The School of Prayer – Practicing Prayer*

> *"Continue steadfastly in prayer,*
> *being watchful in it with thanksgiving."*
> Colossians 4:2

> *"The main lesson about prayer is just this: Do it! Do it!*
> *Do it! You want to be taught to pray. My answer is pray*
> *and never faint, and then you shall never fail..."*
> John Laidlaw – Educator in 1800s

When my daughter Natalie was seven years old and in the second grade, one of her assignments was to write the letters of the alphabet. At that particular time they were working on non-cursive letters, just regular letters, and she had to write them over and over again. Can you imagine if her teacher stood in front of the class and said, "Today I want you to listen to me talk about writing your letters; about how you make the curve on the 'S' and what it looks like." Perhaps she would lecture several hours on writing letters. How much benefit would that be to those children? Probably very little.

As Christians, we talk a lot about prayer. We hear sermons on prayer and think it is wonderful, perhaps in a way you had never thought about before. We talk to other Christians about prayer, we hear people talk about prayer, but we do so little of it. Imagine if a pro-football team adopted this type of practice. They sit in the classroom for hours going over plays. They meet at night to review film. Every chance they get they talk about how much they love football and how important it is in their life. The problem is they never actually practice any of this stuff. Of course that's ridiculous, but it's not much different than how we treat prayer. I'm not sure how much praying you have done during these first 28 days of prayer, but unless I miss my guess, you probably are not happy with the time you've spent in prayer. So, today I want to encourage you to practice praying. Sometimes, tired clichés can be very helpful. Practice is where confidence meets opportunity.

Being intentional is as good as practicing; therefore, I want to give you 10 things to pray for, then I hope you will do that. We're going to use a model of The Lord's Prayer, as well as some other things we've been talking about.

# FIRST

Pray to Your Father in heaven and begin by praising His Name. "Hallowed be Thy Name," pick one of the names of God that maybe you have read about and praise God for who He is.

# SECOND

Pray for Jesus' return. "Thy kingdom come," pray that Jesus will return soon and then make sure you are ready for it. Think about if Jesus were to return today, what needs to happen in your life so that you are ready.

# THIRD

"Thy will be done," pray for His will to be done in your life today. You are asking that He will accomplish what He wants to do through this day He has given to you. And ask that His desires become your desires; that His will becomes your will.

## FOURTH

Pray for your needs. "Give us this day our daily bread." What needs do you have today? What things are on your mind that are overwhelming you? What are those things you want to bring before God?

## FIFTH

Pray for the needs of other people. We looked at Paul and how he prayed for others. He prayed spiritual prayers, "the eyes of your heart may be enlightened" and "you will grow spiritually, understand better who God is and you will walk with Him." Pray prayers for other people to be blessed.

## SIXTH

Pray for our country. Our country needs it. Billy Graham once said, "To get nations back on their feet, we must first get down on our knees." In 1 Timothy, Chapter 2, we are reminded to pray for our leaders.

## SEVENTH

Ask that God would forgive our sins. 1 John 1:9 reminds us to confess our sins and God is faithful and just to forgive us our sins, and cleanse us from all unrighteousness. You need to list your sins and pray, "Lord, I've done this and I know it has broken Your heart; I've done this; I've had this attitude . . ." Ask Him to forgive you of your sins, and while you're doing that, you need to forgive other people, too. You might ask, "Lord, do You find bitterness in me toward anyone? Am I holding a grudge against someone that I'm just hanging on to?" Ask Him to reveal those to you and let that bitterness and those hurt feelings go.

## EIGHTH

Pray like Jabez that God would enlarge your borders. "Lord, give me more influence over this world for You. Give me more influence over people so that I can encourage them to do what is right and know You better."

# NINTH

Pray that God will deliver you from temptation. I can make you a promise today, in the next 24 hours, you will be tempted to sin. You have an enemy, you have the flesh, and you are going to be tempted to sin. You know what some of those temptations are going to be, and you can pray against those specifically. Then pray that God will deliver you from the ones you don't see, and that He will show you a way to escape those temptations, as He promised.

# TENTH

Lastly, praise God's Name again. The Lord's Prayer ends with, "For Thine is the kingdom and the power and the glory forever. Amen." So we end with praising God, lifting up His Name so our focus is on Him when we leave our prayer needs with Him. I hope today you will be intentional in your prayers, and just go talk to God about your needs.

We cannot improve our praying without doing it. We do not just magically become prayer experts when we become Christians. Like anything else in life, we have to work at it to get good at it. It is often said that it takes only 30 days to form a habit. Just do something consistently for one month and it becomes ingrained. Seriously? That's it? Surely you can devote yourselves to praying every day for just 30 days; if you do so, there is a good chance that the habit will stick. Charles Spurgeon characterizes it this way, "Prayer is now as much a necessity of our spiritual life as breath is of our natural life."[1] If we neglect air, we die, if we neglect prayer, we risk dying a much worse death. What are you waiting for? Go practice!

---

1   Robert Hall. *The Power of Prayer in a Believer's Life.* Lynwood: Emerald Books, 1993. 34.

# week 5 | PRAYER EXTINGUISHERS

# DAY 29

*Prayer Extinguishers – Unconfessed Sin*

"Search me oh God and know my heart, test me and know
my anxious thoughts, see if there is any offensive way in
me, and lead me in the way everlasting."
Psalm 139:23-24

"The weeds of unconfessed sin
choke out the life of the soul."
Paul Tripp – Author & Speaker

I remember as a kid my family and I used to go camping. One of the highlights of these camping trips was building a campfire. Anyone who has ever built a fire knows that you can't use wet wood. It just won't catch. Try and try as you might, wet wood will not work for building a campfire. The wood must first be dried out before it will light. Just like the water on that wood, there are certain things in our life that can extinguish our prayers. And we must first learn how to deal with those issues before our prayers can be effective.

## DRYING OUT YOUR WOOD

Sometimes it seems as if God is being silent, and sometimes He really is silent. We're going to explore some things that will cause that to happen. When you feel God's silence, examine yourself in relation to these things and ask, "Is this going on in my life?"

In Job 30:20 we read, "I cry out to you, O God, but you do not answer; I stand up, but you merely look at me." One thing that keeps your wood "wet" according to the Bible, is unconfessed sin in your life. "If I had cherished sin in my heart, the Lord would not have listened." (Psalm 66:18) When you harbor unconfessed sin, you are telling God that you are not going to surrender to Him. In essence, you are disrespecting God. This is made clear throughout the Bible. "The Lord detests the sacrifice of the wicked, but the prayer of the upright pleases him." (Proverbs 15:8)

Are you pursuing His will? Or are you going your own direction, trying to hide your unconfessed sin from the Lord? If you have unconfessed sin in your life, God may not answer your prayers.

## ADMIT YOUR FAULTS

So what should you do? Confess your sin to God. The Bible says, "If we confess our sins, he is faithful and just to forgive us our sins and cleanse us from all unrighteousness." (1 John 1:9) The Bible says that when you turn back to God, He will again hear your prayers. But remember, sincerity is part of the process. Insincere confession is like a teenager who says, "Hey, Dad, I'm sorry I sneaked out last night, I'll never do it again. By the way, could you get those rose bushes trimmed so the next time I won't get all scratched up?" No father is going to buy that because there is no true repentance. Your Father in heaven doesn't buy that either. The Bible says, "If you return to the Almighty, you will be restored; If you remove wickedness far from your tent." (Job 22:23) That key word "far" implies "out of your future reach." That means you have to go back to God and remove the wickedness permanently. If you are willing to repent sincerely, then God is going to hear your prayers. Thus, verbal confession of sin is merely the outward manifestation of the inward reality of repentance of what is in your heart. This means that repentance is something done from the heart. It is a deep realization of your sin and a genuine desire to turn away from it. So you confess your sin and repent of it. Sometimes it may even involve confessing your sin to other people.

James brings this into focus, "Therefore confess your sins to each other and pray for each other so that you may be healed. The prayer of a righteous man is powerful and effective." (James 5:16)

Today will you echo this prayer from the great 19th century pastor Charles Spurgeon with me and begin the journey of confessing sin? "Lord, make us holy. Our prayer comes back to this: make us holy. Cleanse the inside and let the outside be clean, too. Make us holy, O God. Do this for Christ's sake. It is not that we hope to be saved by our own holiness, but holiness is salvation. When we are holy, we are saved from sin."[1]

---

1  Charles Spurgeon, *Spurgeon on Prayer and Spiritual Warfare*, 208.

# DAY 30

*Prayer Extinguishers – Pride*

"For the wicked boasts of the desires of his soul, and the
one greedy for gain curses and renounces the Lord. In
the pride of his face the wicked does not seek him; all his
thoughts are, 'There is no God.'"
Psalm 10:3-4

"It is a big-bellied sin; most of the sins that are in the
world are the offspring and issue of pride."
Richard Mayo – Minister 1600s

ave you ever been driving behind an 18-wheeler? Have you no-
ticed the little picture on the back of most rigs? It's a picture of the
truck with a car pulled up next to it. Then there are two red-dotted
lines that extend down both sides of the truck. These lines indicate the
truck's blind spots. Essentially this picture is a warning to other drivers
that there are certain areas where a truck driver cannot see cars that are
next to him. It's a blind spot, and it's dangerous – very dangerous.

We too have blind spots in our lives. Not the driving kind – the sin
kind. These blind spots keep us from seeing things as they really are and
they are dangerous – very dangerous. Just like unconfessed sin, these
blind spots are prayer extinguishers. One of the most dangerous blind
spots in our lives is pride. The great theologian John Stott once said,

"Pride is our greatest enemy." Today we're going to look at pride and at what pride will do to your prayer life. Job says, "He (God) does not answer when men cry out because of the arrogance of the wicked." (Job 35:12)

God doesn't like it when we are arrogant, but He loves the humble. In Luke 18, Jesus tells the story about two people who go up on a mountain: a Pharisee who was very proud of himself but really a sinner and a tax collector who had swindled some people. The Bible says the Pharisee stood up and prayed about himself, saying, "God, I thank You that I am not like other men – robbers, evildoers, adulterers – or even like this tax collector. I fast twice a week and give a tenth of all I get." But the tax collector stood at a distance. He would not even look up to heaven, but beat his breast and said, "God, have mercy on me, a sinner." In Luke 18:14, Jesus says, "I tell you that this man, rather than the other, went home justified before God. For everyone who exalts himself will be humbled, and he who humbles himself will be exalted."

If our lives are full of pride, there is no room for God. It was the pride of the devil that got him thrown out of heaven, along with one-third of the angels who chose to follow Satan instead of God.

## PRIDE VS. HUMILITY

Pride is the source of so much sin in our lives. Take for example hypocrisy. Pride causes us to hide the truth because we desire for others to see us as better than we are. Or gossip. Pride causes us to speak ill of others in order to feel better about ourselves. What about covetousness? Pride allows you to think that you deserve something more than the other person. It's as Jonathan Edwards once put it, "[Pride] is the main source of all the mischief the devil introduces, to clog and hinder a work of God."[1]

---

1  Jonathan Edwards, "Thoughts on Revival," *Works*, 398-400

If we are going to connect with God, we need to change our prideful nature. Therefore, we have to radically eliminate pride from our lives if we are going to use the power of God's promised blessing. Pride pops up in many different arenas of life. We might be tempted to think highly of ourselves because of our athletic ability, our beauty, our wealth, our brains, our charisma, or even our spiritual accomplishments. Whatever it is, we need to eliminate it from our lives, otherwise God may not hear our prayers, or not answer them.

## THE WORD MAKES YOU HUMBLE

So where do I start? I want to be transformed. I want to be humble in the eyes of God and eliminate my prideful nature. The answer is that when you get into the presence of God, you look at the perfection of God; you study Him, gaze on Him, get your focus on Him. Then you look at the Word of God. Then, you examine yourself. Why would I say "look at the Word of God"? Because the Bible says that God's Word is like a mirror. The Bible says, "Anyone who listens to the word but does not do what it says is like a man who looks at his face in a mirror and, after looking at himself, goes away and immediately forgets what he looks like. But the man who looks intently into the perfect law that gives freedom, and continues to do this, not forgetting what he has heard, but doing it – he will be blessed in what he does." (James 1:23)

God's Word is like a mirror. When you look into it, you see yourself and you know it is you. God's Holy Spirit illuminates His Word. He also illuminates preaching. Sometimes people will comment on a sermon I preach. And I have to say, "Well, I did not mention any of those things you are saying, but the Holy Spirit must have brought those things into focus for you." That is what happens when you get into God's Word. So, James is saying, "Don't forget about what God tells you when you are looking into His Word." It will make you humble.

# GOD USES THE HUMBLE

God uses humble people. He won't use you when you are prideful. David said, "Who am I, O Sovereign Lord, and what is my family that you have brought me this far?" (2 Samuel 7:18)

He says, "Who am I? I'm a shepherd. You made me a king!" His son, Solomon, felt the same way, saying, "Lord, I'm like a little child. I don't know how to go out and come in – why would You use me? Isaiah said, "Woe is me! I'm undone in Your presence." Moses said, "God, I can't speak; go find someone else." Humility is a sign of a true leader – someone God can use. He wants to use you, but He can't if you're proud. What's the solution to our naturally proud hearts? The Bible says,

> "If my people, who are called by my name, will humble themselves and pray and seek my face and turn from their wicked ways, then will I hear from heaven and will forgive their sin and will heal their land."
> (2 Chronicles 7:14)

We have to humble ourselves. That's Plan A. God has a Plan B, though. If we decide not to humble ourselves because we think we are "all that." God says, "Okay, no problem, Plan B."

"The eyes of the arrogant man will be humbled and the pride of men brought low; the Lord alone will be exalted in that day." (Isaiah 2:11)

Why does He say that? Because if you won't humble yourself, God will humble you. The verse above ends with "the Lord alone will be exalted in that day." When we get proud, we are taking away from the glory of God. He is the One to be glorified, not us. Our pride and arrogance robs God of His glory.

So not only will your prayers go unanswered, but God will actually create circumstances that will cause you to be humbled. Jesus put it this way, "Everyone who exalts himself will be humbled; and he who humbles himself will be exalted." (Luke 14:11)

God will exalt you when you humble yourself. God will answer your prayers when you humble yourself. But we have got to be humble. In reality, what do any of us have to be proud of? We possess nothing that we haven't been given by God. So let's thank Him and be humble and praise His Name today.

# DAY 31

*Prayer Extinguishers – Division*

*"The glory that you have given me I have given to them,
that they may be one even as we are one, I in them and
you in me, that they may become perfectly one."*
John 17:22-23

*"Love – and the unity it attests to – is the mark
Christ gave Christians  to wear before the world."*
Francis Schaeffer – Author & Theologian

On June 16, 1858, a tall awkward man stepped onto a stage in Springfield, Illinois to deliver an acceptance speech for the Republican Party's nomination to the United States Senate, "A house divided against itself cannot stand. I believe this government cannot endure, permanently, half slave and half free. I do not expect the Union to be dissolved – I do not expect the house to fall – but I do expect it will cease to be divided." These prophetic words uttered by soon-to-be president Abraham Lincoln eventually rang true.

We've been talking about prayer extinguishers – things in your life that hinder your prayer life. Today we are going to look at one of the often forgotten hindrances to prayer – division. Division amongst people, churches, and groups can arise for any number of reasons. Therefore, we must be careful to see how division creeps in and what we must do in order to keep it from extinguishing our prayer lives.

## BETWEEN FRIENDS

It's amazing how Christians can have a pious look on their faces as they look up toward God, but a hateful and ugly look toward other people. Jesus shines light on this complete inconsistency. "Therefore, if you are offering your gift at the altar and there remember that your brother has something against you, leave your gift there in front of the altar. First go and be reconciled to your brother; then come and offer your gift." (Matthew 5:23-24)

Jesus says not to even bring an offering to God. He doesn't want your offering if you are not living in peace with your brothers and sisters. If they have something against you, go and get it right! You might wonder why you can't have a great relationship just between you and God; that the whole family thing is not that important. That doesn't work. The Bible teaches that we are a family. John says, "Anyone who hates his brother is a murderer, and you know that no murderer has eternal life in him. This is how we know what love is: Jesus Christ laid down his life for us." (1 John 3:15)

He doesn't say Jesus laid His life down for you; he says "us." So if you don't love other people that Jesus laid down His life for, do you really know Him? Are you really in fellowship with Him? John goes a step further and says, "If anyone says 'I love God,' yet hates his brother, he is a liar. For anyone who does not love his brother, whom he has seen, cannot love God, whom he has not seen."

Francis Schaeffer, a theologian, wrote, "We cannot expect the world to believe that the Father sent the Son, that Jesus' claims are true, and that Christianity is true, unless the world sees some reality of the oneness of true Christians."[1] Thus Schaeffer asserts that one of the greatest challenges for Christianity is to fight against division and to seek unity at all costs.

I have four daughters, Natalie, Layla, Reilly, and Abagail. Imagine that we are on our way to get pizza, when suddenly Layla says "shut up!" to her sisters. Next an all out brawl erupts in the back seat. Hitting, kicking, biting, and hair pulling; you know, a little girl brawl. It doesn't matter to me who started it, there had better be some sincere apologies. Or else we are going home to bologna sandwiches and water! I love them all and desire for them to love each other. This is God's point. He loved us enough to send His only Son to die for us. He expects us to love each other. So if there is division, it will hinder our prayers.

# WITHIN THE MARRIAGE

One common place where division pops up is in marriage. What Peter writes concerning prayer might surprise you, "Husbands, in the same way be considerate as you live with your wives, and treat them with respect as the weaker partner and as heirs with you of the gracious gift of life, so that nothing will hinder your prayers." (1 Peter 3:7)

What it says is that God will not answer your prayers if you are not considerate to your wife. She is called "the weaker partner," which means that physically she is weaker. We know very well that it is not referring to intellect or ability. But physically she is weaker. If you fail to be compassionate with her and give her what she needs, the Bible says that God won't answer your prayers. He says that you are both heirs of the "gracious gift of life." He's not talking about the gift of salvation. He's talking about the gift of marriage, which the Bible teaches is the most wonderful relationship as far as earthly human relationships are concerned. Don't mess that up by not being compassionate with your wife. Division in your marriage can cause your prayers not to be heard.

---

1   Francis Schaeffer, *The Mark of the Christian*, 15:1

# UNITY WITHIN THE CHURCH

The third thing that will hinder our prayer life is division in the church. Several years ago the Los Angeles Lakers put together an amazing pro basketball team with Kobe Bryant and Shaquille O'Neal leading the way. The team was unstoppable and it looked as if they would be champs year after year. But division set in between Kobe and Shaq, and the team eventually disintegrated; thus proving the reality that unity is vital for team chemistry. If unity is an essential piece in sports, how much more is it essential for the church?

The church is "the family of God." Anyone who is causing division in the church is definitely going to be at odds with God. If you know a person in the church who is causing problems, perhaps gossiping, saying things they don't know to be true, that person is one whose prayers may not be answered. That person is hurting God's one program on earth to reach the world with the Gospel – the church of Jesus Christ. That's why Paul says, "I appeal to you, brothers, in the name of our Lord Jesus Christ, that all of you agree with one another so that there may be no divisions among you and that you may be perfectly united in mind and thought." (1 Corinthians 1:10)

If you are a person who is causing division in the church – maybe because you think you are more right than your brother – Paul says, "Just agree, be agreeable, get along, don't cause these divisions." God wants us to get along. Now, he's not talking about sacrificing truth, he's talking about divisions that are not really necessary. Get those things out of your life so your prayers can get answered.

Take some time today to evaluate this question: Am I promoting unity in the church? Really look at your life and ask some questions. Is there division in my marriage? Do I have issues with other Christians? If the answer is yes, deal with those issues. Then come to God in prayer when you have eliminated those barriers.

# DAY 32

*Prayer Extinguishers – Saying "No"*

> *"And he did not do many mighty works there,*
> *because of their unbelief."*
> Matthew 13:58

> *"Prayerlessness is the inevitable result of pride or a lack of*
> *faith, usually both. You fail to pray, instinctively,*
> *because you are too proud to realize you need God or too*
> *unbelieving to grasp God's willingness to help."*
> J.D. Greear – Author, Breaking the Islam Code

Everybody knows the word that children learn quickest. Somehow this two-letter word does not need to be taught – it seems innate in their little vocabulary. "NO." It doesn't matter what question you are asking, "no" seems to be the standard response. A lot of times this is how we are with God. "No" seems to be our natural response to the things that God is asking of us. And as we will see today – saying "no" to God can be a major prayer extinguisher.

Have you ever said "no" to God? Maybe you are saying "no" to him right now in a particular area of your life. Maybe you were reading your Bible one day and heard God say, "You should do this," and you thought "Yes, I will!" But you didn't do it. Maybe the Holy Spirit spoke to you and you said "okay" but then you didn't follow through. Maybe you promised to do something for God, or give something to Him. Maybe it was a decision that changed the course of your life, and now you are on a wrong course; and you don't want to get off because it would be too painful. I'm not sure where it was you may have said "no" to God but if your prayer life is extinguished perhaps you should examine this with God.

## THE ROOT OF DISOBEDIENCE

At the root of every "no" response is our unbelief of who God is and what He says. Pastor and author John Piper said, "All the sinful states of our hearts are owing to unbelief in God's super-abounding willingness and ability to work for us in every situation of life so that everything turns out for our good."[1] When we say "no" to God we are saying we don't believe that His intentions and desires are good for our life. When you understand this, it makes sense that saying "no" can be so damaging to your prayer life.

## I WILL OBEY...JUST NOT NOW

It's possible that your answer to God was not an outright "no." Maybe you had a different answer. Maybe God spoke to you clearly and you thought, "That is a great idea! But wait – there's a couple of other things I have to do first. You just wait Your turn, God, and I will get to You."

Jesus told a story about a rich man who decided to throw a banquet and invited three of his friends. "But they all began to make excuses. The first said, 'I have just bought a field, and I must go and see it. Please excuse me.' Another said, 'I have just bought five yoke of oxen, and I'm on my way to try them out. Please excuse me.' Still another said, 'I just got married, so I can't come.'" (Luke 14:18-20)

The first one bought a field he had never seen before? Not a very

---

1 http://www.desiringgod.org/resource-library/sermons/the-perils-of-disapproving-god

smart businessman. The second guy bought five oxen, already purchased them – if they were good, they were good, and if not, they weren't – he could have gone to the supper. The other guy had just gotten married. What? She doesn't eat? Of course, she could have gone with him. These excuses were bogus. The servant knew it. The master knew it. The invitees knew it, but they made excuses. Why? Because they *did* want to go – just not right then. So the servant went back to the master with these excuses and the master said, "Just go out along the streets and the alleys and bring people in so the house will be filled." The servant came back and said, "I did that. I went where you told me, but still there are some empty chairs to be filled." Wouldn't you think that the master would say, "Go back and ask those first three if they want to come now"? But he didn't. Instead, "…the master told his servant, 'Go out to the roads and country lanes and make them come in, so that my house will be full. I tell you, not one of those men who were invited will get a taste of my banquet.'" (Luke 16:23)

Don't be in the habit of telling God to wait. God doesn't want your "wait." Waiting often times is merely a delayed "no." He wants your obedience.

## SO WHAT DO I DO NOW?

How, then, do you get back in line with God where He will hear your prayers and speak to you? First, we must immerse ourselves in the truth of the gospel because it is only when we are reminded of God's infinite love for us that we no longer say "no" or doubt His promises for our lives. The Gospel ultimately shows us that God always did, always does, and always will have our best interests in mind. Therefore, we not only can say "yes," but we can do so with confidence.

Then go back to where you said "no." Remember Jonah? He was a prophet of God and God did use him in a great way. But Jonah told God, "No, I don't want to go to Nineveh. I'm going to Tarshish instead." He got on the boat and trouble followed him. You think it's hard to walk with God, try running from Him! The wind and waves came up around the boat Jonah was on. The crew threw him overboard, then the wind calmed down. But Jonah was still in trouble, he spent three days in the belly of a big fish! Even there God wasn't answering Jonah's prayers until He heard this one – "Okay, Lord, I'm sorry, I'll go." Then, Jonah's fellowship with God was restored. You have to go back to when you said "no" to God to get right with Him.

Today let the power of the Gospel overcome your "no" and then go back to God and make it a "yes." Only then will you experience the prayer life God intended for you.

# DAY 33

*Prayer Extinguishers – Failure to Forgive*

*"Bear with each other and forgive whatever grievances
you may have against one another.
Forgive as the Lord forgave you."*
Colossians 3:13

*"The man who knows he has been forgiven, only in and
through the shed blood of Christ, is a man who must
forgive others. He cannot help himself."*
D.M. Lloyd – Jones Preacher & Medical Doctor

On October 2, 2006, in the morning hours of what seemed to be a regular day of school – Charles Carl Roberts IV walked into an Amish schoolhouse and opened fire on everyone inside. Five schoolgirls died and five others were seriously wounded before Roberts turned the gun on himself.

More stunning than the shooting itself was the response of the Amish community. Many members of the victims' families sought out the shooter's widow and offered forgiveness within days of the trage-dy. One of the families even invited the widow to the funeral of their daughter as a visual sign of forgiveness and reconciliation.

There's something inherently powerful in forgiveness. As one commentator notes, "Forgiveness is almost a single-word summary of both the Christian Gospel and of the Christian ethic, of God's gift to us and our responsibility to others."[1]

Today we'll look at how the failure to forgive can extinguish your prayers. I don't want you to think that there is a list of hundreds of things that can kill your prayers – as if God is waiting to zap your prayers because He doesn't like some things you did. That is not the case. But failure to forgive is something that will zap your prayers. The Bible says, "Be kind and compassionate to one another, forgiving each other, just as in Christ God forgave you." (Ephesians 4:32)

## A CHANGE OF HEART

Forgiveness is one of the truest indications of our understanding of the Gospel. You are supposed to forgive people just like God forgave you. When God forgave you, it was just like the prodigal son coming home. He was walking down a long road home, wondering what it would be like when his dad saw him. Dad would probably call him names and let him know what an embarrassing disappointment he had been. These were probably the son's thoughts on that long journey home. When he got home, though, his dad saw him from a long distance away. He ran to his son and embraced him. He put a ring on his finger and shoes on his feet. The son got a new robe and a party thrown in his honor. All was forgiven. That is how God forgave me, and that's how He forgave you. How willing are we to forgive like that? That's how willing we ought to be to forgive others.

Peter asked, "How often should I forgive my brother? Should I forgive him seven times?" When he asked Jesus this question, he thought he was shooting for the stars! The average Jew was told to forgive three times and after that – justice! The boot! No more forgiveness from me! So when Peter said seven, he thought he was being gracious. But Jesus

---

1   Frederick Dale Bruner, *The Christbook* – Matthew 1-12.

said, "Oh, no, not seven; seventy times seven," a number far beyond the standard. Forgive every time your brother asks you for forgiveness.

And how do we know when we've forgiven them? Thomas Watson, the great Puritan, answered the question this way, "When we strive against all thoughts of revenge; when we will not do our enemies mischief, but wish well to them, grieve at their calamities, pray for them, seek reconciliation with them, and show ourselves ready on all occasions to relieve them."[2] Forgiveness is, therefore, a heart change. Jesus is not concerned with the number of times we forgive, but rather with the condition of our hearts when we forgive.

# GRACE

Now, if you say, "I refuse to forgive," what happens then? Jesus tells us in the Lord's Prayer that if you do not forgive men their sins, your Father will not forgive your sins.

If you do not forgive others, you are going to have a blockage between you and God. You will hinder your relationship with God. He is still your Father. When you accept Jesus into your life, judicially your sins have been forgiven once and for all. In other words, you will receive eternal life in Heaven and never answer for those sins on judgment day. But when you don't forgive, the relationship between you and God is damaged and your prayers will not be answered.

Even if you've been maligned or molested, it doesn't make it right to not forgive. In fact, you are the one who bears that burden. There might be someone you just hate. Your hatred for them may have no effect on that person, but it might affect other people in your life, probably people you love. The Bible says, "See to it that no one misses the grace of God and that no bitter root grows up to cause trouble and defile many." (Hebrews 12:15)

---

2   Thomas Watson, *Body of Divinity*, 581.

If you have bitterness in your life, it defiles your family. You may have heard this saying, "Hurt people hurt people." You hurt your family, your spouse, your loved ones, your co-workers – anyone close to you.

Grace is defined as giving someone something good they don't deserve. Everybody wants grace from God. But we are all reluctant to give it out.

Forgiveness is never an easy task – regardless of what someone might think. It forces us to put aside our pride and humble ourselves, sometimes in the midst of enormous pain and hurt. However, we must look to the cross where Christ endured a horrible death as an innocent man so that we could be forgiven. Our ability to look to the cross and grasp the love of God for us will translate into our ability to forgive others even of the most horrendous acts. Today, don't let a lack of forgiveness get in the way of your prayer life. Go and forgive just as you have been forgiven.

# DAY 34

*Prayer Extinguishers – Idolatry*

*"I am the Lord your God, who brought you out of the land*
*of Egypt, out of the house of slavery. You shall have no*
*other gods before me."*
*Exodus 20:2-3*

*"What the prohibition of idolatry in the second*
*commandment implies is that God's people should*
*be positively and passionately devoted to his person,*
*his cause and his honor."*
*J.I. Packer – Theologian*

When "things" and/or personal gratification become our highest priority, there is a good chance we are heading for idolatry. Take money for example. Money is obviously a necessary part of our everyday lives. But when we make money the thing we live for – always needing more and never having enough – it becomes a higher priority than it ought to be. When this happens with money – or anything else – it turns into an idol.

For the past few days we've been looking at numerous ways in which our prayers can be extinguished because of various sins in our lives. Today we look at another prayer extinguisher – idolatry (or false gods). Many people might think, "Well I don't worship idols (or false gods). The reality is, anytime we replace God (the Creator) with something

He has made (the creation), we are worshiping an idol. And anytime we are worshiping an idol, our prayer lives are drastically hindered. God explicitly says, "You shall have no other gods before me." (Exodus 20:3)

## ASK YOUR "NEW" GOD FOR HELP

You might be surprised at how upset God gets when we replace Him with an idol. Look at what He says, "I will bring on them a disaster they cannot escape. Although they cry out to me, I will not listen to them. The towns of Judah and the people of Jerusalem will go and cry out to the gods to whom they burn incense, but they will not help them at all when disaster strikes. You have as many gods as you have towns, O Judah; and the altars you have set up to burn incense to that shameful god Baal are as many as the streets of Jerusalem. Do not pray for this people nor offer any plea or petition for them, because I will not listen when they call to me in the time of their distress." (Jeremiah 11:11) God says don't bother asking Me for help when things fall apart, ask your new gods to save you.

## IDOLS ARE NOT A NEW PROBLEM

In the Old Testament and the New Testament, there were many false gods that were worshipped. There was Baal, Asherah, Baal-peor, Kimosh, Dagon, Diana and Molech. The people would take a block of wood and carve an idol to worship. There's nothing wrong with the block of wood. God made the tree. But the people made something evil out of something good. Today's idols may look a little different, but we do the same thing.

Tim Keller writes, "To contemporary people the word idolatry conjures up pictures of primitive people bowing down before statues...but our contemporary society is not fundamentally different from these ancient ones. Each one has its own shrines – whether office towers, spas and gyms, studios, or stadiums – where sacrifices must be made in order to procure blessings of the good life and ward off disaster. What are the gods of beauty, power, money, and achievement but these same things that have assumed mythic proportions in our individual lives and in our society?"[1]

## QUESTION: WHERE CAN IDOLS BE FOUND TODAY?

We take things that aren't bad, maybe even necessary, but we can turn those things into gods. What is the definition of a false god? Anything that we trust to meet our needs and bring us happiness, security, prosperity and quality of life. Sometimes people can become false gods in our lives. It can be children, your spouse, a friend, or a group of friends. It might even be your parents from whom you've never really cut loose the apron strings. Those people can all be primary sources of security to you, when God should be your primary source of security.

Sometimes worldly possessions become our gods. It might be a boat, a car, a house, a bank account, maybe a job, IRA, money market account, mutual funds, gold, jewelry, an inheritance, a trust, some property, or maybe a settlement you hope to get. No matter what form, the worship of worldly possessions can bring us down. Jesus put it this way, "No one can serve two masters. Either he will hate the one and love the other, or he will be devoted to the one and despise the other. You cannot serve both God and money." (Matthew 6:24)

A rich man once asked Jesus what he needed to do to have eternal life. Jesus answered, "If you want to be perfect, go, sell your possessions and give to the poor, and you will have treasure in heaven. Then come, follow me." (Matthew 19:21-22) Jesus said you have to choose either Me or your stuff. The Bible says he walked away sad. He chose his possessions over Jesus. Since money was his god, he chose to trust and obey it rather than Jesus.

---

1  Timothy Keller, *Counterfeit Gods*, xii.

# DETHRONING THE IDOL

Idols come in many forms – possessions, sexual immorality, reputation, good looks, leisure, sports. We can make an idol out of almost anything. What do we do to deal with these current day idols? How do you de-throne a false god?

Again, Tim Keller is helpful in suggesting an answer, "Jesus must become more beautiful to your imagination, more attractive to your heart, than your idol. That is what will replace your counterfeit gods. If you uproot the idol and fail to 'plant' the love of Christ in its place, the idol will grow back."[2] Thus Keller asserts that replacing idols involves both repentance and rejoicing. We must both turn away from our idols and turn towards God. This usually involves fellowship, prayer, service, study, giving, as well as obedience.

You need to put Jesus on the throne of your life. When He is your God, your Trust, your Source of security, the One you know will meet your needs, these other false idols are going to fade away.

---

2    Timothy Keller, *Counterfeit Gods*, 172.

# DAY 35

*Prayer Extinguishers – Grumbling*

"Rejoice in the Lord always; again, I will say rejoice."
Philippians 4:4

"Many men think that when they are troubled and have
not got contentment, it is because they have but a little in
the world, and if they had more then they
would be content...No, the reason is because
the thing is not suitable to a craving stomach."
Jeremiah Burroughs – English Congregationalist 1600s

Living in Fresno, sunglasses are a necessity. Sunglasses for Fresnans are like umbrellas for Seattle residents. Every day when I get home, I put my sunglasses in the same place right beside the door. And every morning when I leave I pick them up on my way out. Now there are certain days when I get in my car and put my sunglasses on and everything I see is blurry. I immediately know that one of children has been playing with my sunglasses because their little fingerprints are all over them. As a result I see everything though messed up lenses. Everything looks a bit gloomier and dingier until I clean them off.

This is how the next prayer extinguisher works in our hearts. Grumbling skews the way we perceive everything. Instead of finding joy in life – persons who indulge in grumbling find a problem with just about anything. Therefore it stands to reason that our prayer life doesn't have a chance if we are constantly grumbling.

## COUNT YOUR BLESSINGS

In 1 Corinthians 10:1-4 we read, "For I do not want you to be ignorant of the fact, brothers and sisters, that our ancestors were all under the cloud and that they all passed through the sea. They were all baptized into Moses in the cloud and in the sea. They all ate the same spiritual food and drank the same spiritual drink; for they drank from the spiritual rock that accompanied them, and that rock was Christ."

In this passage we learn that God provided food, drink, safety, and guidance for the Israelites when they were wandering in the wilderness. They were privileged people who saw God's miraculous power when He parted the Red Sea.

They drank water from a rock; Christ was accompanying them on this journey across the wilderness. Look at what Paul says next in verse 5, "Nevertheless, God was not pleased with most of them; their bodies were scattered in the wilderness." Whoa! Hold on a minute! What did they do? They were idolaters, they were sexually immoral. Verse 10 continues, "And do not grumble, as some of them did – and were killed by the destroying angel."

## CONTENTMENT OR BITTERNESS

The Israelites were grumbling and God let their bodies be scattered all over the desert because of it! Incredible! What were they complaining about? They were grumbling about what God had provided for them – the manna; they were sick of it. They wanted leeks and garlics from Egypt. Imagine that kind of attitude when God was providing for them. However, we do the very same thing. A "never-satisfied" attitude seems to be the driving force of our society. God provides us with a place to live, a car, food, and still we grumble about wanting better food, a better car, wishing for more money to pay for the house and do things we want to do. We grumble, and God hates it. He hates complaining. So today I want to show you how you can learn to stop grumbling.

At the heart of grumbling is a lack of contentment. First, you have to learn contentment. "But godliness with contentment is great gain." (1 Timothy 6:6) It's great gain not to make a lot of money; great gain not to have a successful business with perpetuity in your income or multiple strains of income – that's not it. Contentment and being Godly is great gain. Verse 7 says, "For we brought nothing into the world, and we can take nothing out of it." You are not going to take your 401K to heaven, so stop worrying about it. Turn off MSNBC or CNBC or whatever ticker you are watching, just so you can worry about your future. Your future is in God's hands and you will be taking none of your earthly gains with you. Verse 8: "But if we have food and clothing, we will be content with that." We need to be content with the basic necessities of life because we have Jesus – and He is all you need. Do you believe this? If not you need to learn contentment.

## GIVE THANKS

Secondly, you need to learn to be thankful. We've talked about that before. We looked at Psalm 100:4 where David says, "Enter into his gates with thanksgiving and his courts with praise." Give thanks to Him and praise His Name. When you begin your prayer, start with gratitude. Gratefulness for who God is and what He has done. We hallow His Name, as we talked about in The Lord's Prayer, and we are also grateful for what He has done, and what our Father has given to us. List 10 or 15 things every day when you wake up – things to be thankful for – sunlight, life, a wonderful family – begin to be grateful for the things God has given you.

## BE GENEROUS

Last, learn to give. Nothing will break the hold of selfishness and grumbling like giving. It is almost impossible to be giving and to be ungrateful and grumbling at the same time. The Bible teaches that if we see brothers in need and we don't give them what they need, we might as well not have any faith at all. Look around today at the needs of others and see what you can do to help. You can't meet all their needs, but there are some you can meet. And that will break the back of grumbling in your life.

Today start by taking off the blurry sunglasses causing you to see life through the skewed lenses of grumbling. Repent of the ways in which you have not found contentment in Christ. Then write out a list of all the things you have to be thankful for. Then sit down and think about one way you can meet someone's need today. As you apply these concepts in your life, watch and see how your prayer life is freed from the tyranny of grumbling.

# week 6 | TIME & PRAYER

# DAY 36

*Time & Prayer – Taking Time to Pray*

*"The widow who is really in need and left all alone puts her hope in God and continues night and day to pray and to ask God for help."*
1 Timothy 5:5

*"Time spent alone with God is not wasted. It changes us; it changes our surroundings; and every Christian who would live the life that counts, and who would have power for service must take time to pray."*
M.E. Andross – The Prayer Motivator

If I had to guess, the number one reason why many people say they don't pray is because they don't have time. After taking the kids to school, working all day, finding time to exercise, making dinner, cleaning up the house, and watching your favorite shows on television, there is just no time left to pray.

Now imagine for a second that you treated eating the same way you treated prayer. You knew you should do it but it was just one of those things that you couldn't find time for. Sure you'd sneak a quick snack in here and there. But you just didn't have any time to sit down and have a nice meal. Eventually your body would begin to deteriorate and you would die. This is exactly what's happening to your soul when you fail to pray. You are slowly allowing the things of this world to consume you, and it causes your spiritual life to slowly deteriorate until the point of spiritual death.

If you didn't drink water for a week, you would be dead! Not having time is really not a good excuse for not eating or drinking. If you decide you don't have time to sleep and you go 40 days without sleep, you'll die. Physically, you can't live that long without sleep. It's like saying you're going to take a trip across country, but you don't want to take the time to fuel up. That's not very logical. You're going to run out of gas. It's like a battle that you have to fight right now, but you don't have time to make a plan. That is also ludicrous. In the same way, we have to pray. And we have to pray effectively; going through the motions of prayer, but thinking about all of the other things we could be doing is not praying. Prayer is the work we should be doing!

## TAKE TIME

Peter Kreeft says regarding prayer, "The hardest thing, and the most essential thing of all...is simply taking time to pray...It's the most essential thing of all just because its not a matter of how you do it at all, but of whether you do it. Like being born, or cooking: How you do it is less important than whether you do it. You can find thousands of books on prayer that give you methods of praying, hundreds of 'hows'; but they do you no good at all unless you actually pray. Otherwise, it's just like reading a cookbook instead of cooking. You can't eat a cookbook!"[1]

## CHOOSE YOUR WORDS

The emphasis in Scripture is not on praying with a lot of words. Jesus said, "And when you pray, do not keep on babbling like pagans, for they think they will be heard because of their many words." (Matthew 6:7) It's not many words that make us heard. In fact it is often the opposite. Solomon put it this way, "Do not be quick with your mouth, do not be

---

1   Peter Kreeft, Prayer: *The Great Conversation*, 12.

hasty in your heart to utter anything before God. God is in heaven and you are on earth, so let your words be few." (Ecclesiastes 5:2) This means that when you get before God, don't go off on a tangent and talk, talk, talk.

The emphasis is on quality, not quantity; on what you say, not how much you say. You might think you're being nice to me by giving me an unlimited supply of red licorice. But since I hate licorice, it doesn't matter how much you give me, I won't eat it. I'd rather eat one piece of caramel than a hundred pieces of licorice. The same is true for prayer. God would rather hear a few words that reveal our hearts than a thousand words that merely put on a show.

## INCLUDE TIME FOR LISTENING

God wants to talk to you, too! Have you ever been with someone who won't let you get a word in edgewise? Pretty soon, you just give up – talking and listening! God must feel like that with us sometimes, because we just talk. Get into His presence and let your words be few. Think about what you are going to say and listen for His voice.

## PRAY OFTEN

There is another thing spoken of in Scripture regarding prayer – frequency. Be in God's presence, many, many, many times during the day. The Bible says, "O Lord, the God who saves me, day and night I cry out before you." (Psalm 88:1) Paul simply says, "Pray continually." (1 Thessalonians 5:17)

How can we accomplish this? How can you have consistency in your prayer life? Do you just say, "I'll try to do that more often?" Is that going to work? Not really.

First, you have to go back to the Gospel. Remember what we said back in Week 1 about why we don't pray? We don't pray because we don't believe God's promise to hear us and answer our prayers. So first we have to remember that in Christ, God has demonstrated His love for us and His desire to communicate with us. It is in response to this love that we desire to pray more consistently – to make prayer an integral part of our day.

## PRAY WITH A PLAN

But it's also helpful if you see prayer like budgeting. A budget is a plan – so much for rent, so much for food, so much for clothes. If prayer is going to be a big part of your life, and if this *40 Days of Prayer* is going to have any impact on your life, you have to make a plan. You need to plan times to pray, like Daniel did. The Bible says about Daniel, "Three times a day he got down on his knees and prayed, giving thanks to his God..." (Daniel 6:10)

In other words, Daniel had a plan. Every day, without fail, he prayed – morning, noon and night. That was how he lived. It was a plan he developed. David says, "Evening, morning and noon I cry out in distress and he hears my voice." (Psalm 55:17)

This is a pattern. You want to start in the morning. David says in Psalm 5:3, "In the morning, O Lord, you hear my voice; in the morning I lay my requests before you and wait in expectation."

The morning is a great time to pray because you have your whole day ahead of you and you can lay before the Lord what your needs are for the day. Wherever your temptations are going to be, you can pray He will lead you out of those. You are free from the distractions of the day's business because the day's business hasn't started. Pray for your daily needs. Pray His Name will be lifted high in your life and that His will be done in your life; that His kingdom will come. These are things you can pray for every day, starting in the morning. Then at noon, the whole morning has gone and a lot has happened. You can pray about what has happened and about the rest of the day to come. You take a break at midday and get back with the Lord again.

Then you also pray at the end of the day. "On my bed I remember you; I think of you through the watches of the night." (Psalm 63:6) Again David says," I rise before dawn and cry for help; I have put my hope in your word. My eyes stay open through the watches of the night." (Psalm 119:147-148)

So you end your day in prayer also. God wants us to be in His presence morning, noon, and night. Remember, it's not a matter of how you do it, but rather that you do it. Begin today to plan a time and place in the morning, a time and a place in the afternoon, and a time and a place in the evening. I hope you will make this plan for your life right now.

# DAY 37

*Time & Prayer – The Hour of Prayer*

> *"For a day in your courts is better than a*
> *thousand elsewhere."*
> Psalm 84:10

> *"Sweet hour of prayer! Sweet hour of prayer!*
> *That calls me from a world of care,*
> *And bids me at my Father's throne*
> *Make all my wants and wishes known."*
> William Walford – Author of Hymn Sweet Hour of Prayer

A good friend of mine once told me that while in college, he would have to drive several hours every other weekend to visit his wife (then girlfriend). The drive to her place was easy because he was so excited to see her. But the drive home was the worst. Since they didn't see each other that much, they would hang out until the last minute Sunday night. That meant my friend would have to drive late at night. The route home was mostly back woods so there was not a whole lot to keep his attention. My friend said it was the hardest thing to do to stay awake. He would blast the music, put all the windows down, and drink a big coffee. But he said his body still just wanted to sleep.

Have you ever felt this way in prayer? It could be the middle of the day and you haven't felt tired all day. But as soon as you go to pray, you find yourself dozing off. I know I have! And the disciples did as well.

Jesus found His disciples asleep in the Garden of Gethsemane. He had asked them to pray for Him, but they fell asleep. He asked them a question they never forgot. "Could you men not keep watch with me for one hour?" (Matthew 26:40) Jesus was saying, "Here I am being crucified tomorrow – is one hour too much to ask?"

Yesterday, we said the issue is not the amount of time you pray. God doesn't need for you to talk a lot, but being in His presence for any length of time will do amazing things for your life. Today we are going to talk about how you can do that. I would like to present one possible plan to you from Dick Eastman, who wrote a book entitled *The Hour That Changes The World*. He describes a way you can pray for an hour in 12 periods of about five minutes each. As you become more comfortable praying about each segment, it will be a challenge to contain all you want to say in five minutes per segment. Once you do this a few times, you may not want to go back to your old prayer life.

1. **Start your prayer with praise and worship.** The Bible says, "Not to us, O Lord, not to us but to your name be the glory, because of your love and faithfulness." (Psalm 115:1) Just as in the Lord's Prayer when you start by hallowing God's Name and praising His Name, you will start this prayer by lifting Him up. He is your Creator, how could you not praise Him? He is your Savior, the One who has given you salvation. He is a great God; He is omnipresent, omniscient, all-knowing, He is amazing! Pick a different theme of praise each time you pray.

2. **Wait on the Lord.** This is an act of surrender and love. When you are in the Lord's presence, spend some time in silence. The Bible says, "Be still, and know that I am God..." (Psalm 46:10) Just be in God's presence; knowing He is there; knowing you are with Him. Experience His love and surrender to Him in those moments. It gets you ready for the rest of your prayer time.

3. **Confession**. This is a time of introspection, when you say, "Search me, O God; know my heart; know my thoughts; and if there is any wicked way in me; test me where I am anxious," (Psalm 139:23) Confess any sins to the Lord as it says in 1 John 1:9, "If we confess our sins, he is faithful and just and will forgive us our sins and purify us from all unrighteousness." It is only because of the cross that we can be forgiven.

4. **Pray Scripture**. That means you take your Bible and pray back to God what you read. You might find a warning and say, "Lord, keep me from this." You might find a promise and say, "Lord, I claim this promise." You might say, "Lord, thank You for the faithfulness You showed to Hannah when You gave her that baby boy." Or "Lord, thank You for how You delivered David from Goliath, from the bear, from the lion." Whatever you find, just talk it back to God. That is praying scripture.

5. **Watch**. The Bible says in Colossians 4:2, "Devote yourselves to prayer, being watchful and thankful." Watching means you are going to ask the Lord, "What is it that I have to watch out for in my life spiritually? What are the things that could come into my life and trip me up? What is going on that I am not seeing?" The things that are unseen are just as real as the things that are seen. They may even be more real. "Lord, help me to see the unseen." That's watching.

6. **Intercede**. 1 Timothy 2:1-2, "I urge, then, first of all, that requests, prayers, intercession and thanksgiving be made for everyone – for kings and all those in authority, that we may live peaceful and quiet lives in all godliness and holiness." We pray for other people, other believers, those in authority – we intercede for them. Later we'll talk about a prayer list, but you might need to make a list for intercession because there are so many people who need our prayer.

7. **Petition.** This is asking for things you need. "Give us this day our daily bread." You only have five minutes in this 60 minutes of prayer to pray for yourself – better make it quick.

8. **Give thanks.** 1 Thessalonians 5:18, "Give thanks in all circumstances, for this is God's will for you in Christ Jesus." God's will is that you are thankful, so take five minutes of your prayer time and express your thankfulness for what He has done in your life; for what He has done for you.

9. **Sing.** Psalm 100 talks about this. This is serious! You are probably snickering, saying, "God doesn't want to hear my song." But He does! "Shout for joy to the Lord, all the earth. Worship the Lord with gladness; come before him with joyful songs." You can make up songs, or sing a song you know. Find a solitary place where you can be alone and just pray and sing to the Lord. It will change your worship.

10. **Meditate.** Psalm 1:1-2, "Blessed is the man who does not walk in the counsel of the wicked or stand in the way of sinners or sit in the seat of mockers. But his delight is in the law of the Lord, and on his law he meditates day and night." You are going to be firmly established in your faith when you meditate on the Lord. Think about Him; think about who He is; think about obedience to Him; maybe take a portion of Scripture and meditate on it for five minutes. Meditate on God in His presence.

11. **Listen.** Ecclesiastes 5:2, "Do not be quick with your mouth, do not be hasty in your heart to utter anything before God. God is in heaven and you are on earth, so let your words be few." In other words, listen to God. You will be amazed how God can speak to you.

12. **Praise.** We end our prayer with praise, just as in The Lord's Prayer, Matthew 6:13, (King James Version) "And lead us not

into temptation, but deliver us from evil, for Thine is the king-dom and the power and the glory forever, in Jesus' Name, Amen." End your prayer by thanking God for who He is and praising God for who He is.

Remember my friend who had trouble staying awake while driving home? Remember how on his way to his girlfriend's he didn't have any trouble staying awake? Well, my hope is that these 12 prayer tips will help make your prayer life more like his trip to his girlfriend's house. When we learn how to pray and learn its importance for our lives, we can get excited! That excitement can help us fight against the distractions we face while praying. So today, give these 12 prayer periods a try and allow your time in prayer to increase.

# DAY 38
*Time & Prayer – Praying without Ceasing*

*"Always keep on praying."*
1 Thessalonians 5:17

*"If the spiritual life be healthy, under the full power of the
Holy Spirit, praying without ceasing will be natural."*
*Andrew Murray – South African Pastor & Teacher*

Dean Karnazes is an ultra marathoner. What's an ultra marathon you ask? It is roughly defined as any race that eclipses the 26.2 mile marathon mark. Most ultra marathons range somewhere between 50 to 200 miles. Karnazes himself has run dozens of these, including the 135-mile Death Valley race, a 200-mile relay by himself, and has topped it all with a 350-mile run. What's even more grueling about these races is the time frame in which they are run. Many are run within 24-48 hours. Some of the longest, however, can stretch for 3-6 days. It is literally running without ceasing.

Paul advocates a similar marathon in 1 Thessalonians 5:17 – the ultra prayer marathon. He recommends a prayer life that does not stop at 26.2 miles but continues daily, weekly, monthly. Prayer without ceasing.

Surely Paul cannot expect us to do that...can he?

One day Nehemiah, a prophet, was called to stand before King Artaxerxes. Nehemiah was sad. It could be a death sentence if you went before the king sad, because the King had enough on his mind without having to be concerned with anyone else's worries. The king asked Nehemiah, "Why are you sad?" And Nehemiah said, "The gates of my hometown in Jerusalem are broken down." And the king asked, "What do you want?" The Bible says Nehemiah prayed. Did he get down on his knees? No. It was that quick prayer to the Lord, "Lord, help me! Give me the words to say! Give me wisdom!" Nehemiah knew the power of prayer without ceasing.

In John 15, Jesus called this "abiding in him." In the late 1600s, a devout Christian, Brother Lawrence, wrote articles on what he called *Practicing the Presence of God.* In one of these he said, "I write this only because you have so earnestly requested that I explain to you the method by which I have learned how to develop an habitual sense of God's presence, which our Lord, in his mercy, has been pleased to grant me."

What does it mean to abide in Christ, or practice the presence of God, or pray without ceasing? It is a continuous, deliberate fellowship with the Father that involves four activities.

## FOCUS ON GOD

First and foremost is focus. You are going to focus on God all day long, and talk to Him, (pray) all day long. The Bible doesn't really describe the length of your individual prayers, but focuses more on the frequency of your prayers. We are told to pray all the time. This is not necessarily a formal time of prayer. Rather it is your soul's constant communication with your Heavenly Father – expressing your thanksgiving to Him, repenting of sin, and offering up requests.

## LISTENING TO GOD

Secondly, listening to God, hearing His voice. In John 10, Jesus said, "My sheep hear my voice and they obey me." So, we are listening for His voice, to help us be obedient and to align ourselves with His will.

## THINK ABOUT GOD

Thirdly, we need to meditate on Him; always thinking on Him and what He says to say and do. In The Lord's Prayer, we begin with "Hallowed be your name." We talked before about the names of God. You are thinking about His attributes, His Name and who He is. This will result in amazing things in your life and will continually bolster your faith.

## THINK ABOUT GOD'S WORD

Fourthly, when you are praying without ceasing, you are fixating on God's Word. His Word is what we get into our hearts to replace the things of this world. We will then begin to hear His voice, which the Bible says allows the Holy Spirit to bring His Word back to our mind.

## WHAT CAN I EXPECT?

What happens to a person who prays without ceasing? First of all, he has great peace. "Great peace have they who love your law (His Word), and nothing can make them stumble." (Psalm 119:165) If you are meditating on God's Word, you are going to have great peace.

Next, you become more fruitful. Jesus said, "I am the vine; you are the branches. If a man remains in me and I in him, he will bear much fruit; apart from me you can do nothing." (John 15:5) You will be fruitful when you abide in Christ, because you are thinking His thoughts about His word. Hence, what you say or do is a reflection of Christ; you become a light for others. As people gravitate around you, your opportunity to share Christ grows geometrically.

Next, you will become prosperous. In others words, God will bless your life. In fact God promised that if we would meditate on His word He would make us "prosperous and successful." (Joshua 1:8) That is a huge promise, and even repeated in the Bible. David talks about the person who meditates on God's word; saying, "He is like a tree planted by streams of water, which yields its fruit in season and whose leaf does not wither. Whatever he does prospers!" (Psalm 1:3)

Lastly, you begin living in the moment. You're not thinking about the failures or successes of the past. You are not concerned about the problems or the pleasures of the future. You will think about the present, because you are going to see all the immediate needs in front of you through God's eyes. Hence, you are constantly bringing those things before God because you are in constant contact with Him.

Your sinful nature is not going to let you pray without ceasing without a fight. Your flesh is going to say, "I don't want to pray! I don't want to think about God!" And you are going to have a fight on your hands as you begin this process. But fight that fight, it is worth it in the end.

So I encourage you today to begin a new life – a life of ultra-prayer. Enter into His presence and enter into a relationship with Him where you pray without ceasing. He will change your life and you will never regret it.

# DAY 39

*Time & Prayer – Making a Prayer List*

*"We give thanks to God always for you all, making mention of you in our prayers; Remembering without ceasing your work of faith, and labour of love, and patience of hope in our Lord Jesus Christ, in the sight of God and our Father."*
1 Thessalonians 1:2-3

*"The bottom line is we don't write down our prayer requests because we don't take prayer seriously. We don't think it works."*
Paul Miller – Author, A Praying Life

If there is one thing I hate it is grocery shopping. I am terrible at it. Now I know you're thinking: "Will, how can you be bad at grocery shopping?" My ability to grocery shop is measured by my ability to remember what I'm shopping for. And since I forget at least half of the items my wife asks me to get; I consider myself a bad grocery shopper. However, some people are great grocery shoppers. Why? They make meticulous lists with prioritized items. Therefore, they never forget anything they set out to get.

The same can be true for our prayer life. It can be less than productive when we set out to pray and forget half the things we wanted to pray for. But there's a better way. Make a list! Simple, huh? It is simple but revolutionary for your prayer life. Today we're going to take a look at what that list could look like.

# PRAY FOR LEADERS

Paul says, "I urge, then, first of all, that requests, prayers, intercession and thanksgiving be made for everyone – for kings and all those in authority, that we may live peaceful and quiet lives in all godliness and holiness." (1 Timothy 2:1-2)

In our case, we don't have a king, but our President deserves our prayer every day, according to God's Word. Pray he will make right decisions. He won't every time, no one does. But we pray for him and for salvation and that he comes to know Jesus Christ in a personal way. We do that for all those in authority.

Make a list of those who are in authority. Go on-line and get the names of world leaders in different countries, national leaders in our country, local leaders in your state and community. Pray for each one frequently – if not every day, then at least weekly. But your list should include people who are in authority. Why? First and foremost, praying for world leaders causes us to remember who is in control. We are reminded that no matter how powerful a world leader might be, God is still sovereign and we need Him to intercede on our behalf. Then from here we can pray, "That we may live peaceful lives." (1 Timothy 2:2) We pray that leaders will bring peace in our land and in the world.

The Apostle Paul lived at a time when the person on the throne was not a very good person; actually, he was a pedophile. Yet Paul says here that you need to give him honor. Jesus said, "Give to Caesar what is Caesar's." Paul says in Romans 13:1 that we need to obey all authorities. Whoever they are, we need to pray for them.

# PRAY FOR FAMILY

In addition to leaders, pray for your family. In the Bible there are all kinds of people who prayed for their families. Isaac's servant prayed He would find him the right wife. People were praying for the health of those in their family. Put your family on that prayer list and pray for them every day. And pray spiritual requests, not just for health or that they get a job, but pray, "Lord, I pray my dad would have a walk with You that is vibrant today. I pray that my daughter would come to know You in a very real way and understand how You work in her life."

## PRAY FOR FRIENDS

Next, pray for your friends, pray for your church and for your church staff. List those staff members by name and pray for a different one each day.

Here are some other items to add to a prayer list: Pray for missionaries across the world spreading the gospel to unreached people groups. Pray for lost people in your neighborhood and opportunities to share the Gospel. Pray for your work (even if your work is at home with your kids) and that God would be glorified in your work. Be creative and don't worry about the list being too long.

Your prayer list is going to deepen your prayer life. Pray without a list and you are going to pray for whatever comes into your mind at the moment. A list gives an order to your prayers and helps you pray for a particular person; let's say your mother-in-law. If she's on your list you'll say, "Lord, I want to pray for this person." Then pause. Let the Lord speak to you about how to pray for her. Give the Lord some latitude to bring things to your mind.

George Mueller, that 1800s evangelist I have previously cited, had a prayer list with over 10,000 people and things on it that he prayed for in his lifetime. When he got an answer to a prayer, he would write "answered" next to it. Can you imagine what that would do for your faith to see all those "answered" notations next to your prayer requests? I want to encourage you to do that. Get a notebook, sit down and list people and their prayer requests. Keep that notebook with you. Once a day, write down your prayer requests, making the requests specific enough so that you can write "answered" next to them. You will be amazed at how your list and your faith will grow.

# DAY 40

## Time & Prayer – Leaving a Legacy

*"These words that I command you today shall be
on your heart. You shall teach them diligently to
your children, and shall talk of them when you
sit in your house, and when you walk by the way,
and when you lie down, and when you rise."*
*Deuteronomy 6:6-7*

*"I would rather teach one man
to pray than ten men to preach."*
*Charles Spurgeon – Pastor & Author 1800s*

When I was in seminary I had a professor who was known for prayer. He even taught a class entitled "Prayer." He was constantly asking students how he could pray for them. The professor's name was Dr. Roscup. Prayer was his legacy. Today I want to close out our 40 days by talking about how you can leave a legacy of prayer.

## WHAT WILL THEY SAY ABOUT YOU?

Do you know that God saves your prayers? You have never breathed a prayer up to the Lord that He did not save. The Bible teaches in Revelation 5:8 that one day the prayers of the saints will be released in heaven as a sweet fragrance to the Lord. You can leave a legacy for prayer by your reputation for prayer. Many people in the Bible did that. Hannah was known for her prayer for a son. David was known for his prayers in the book of Psalms. Jabez was known for a mighty prayer that God answered. What do you think you are known for? What would be written on your tombstone if you were to die today? I enjoy football, but I don't want that on my tombstone. I hope that I leave a legacy for living a more significant life than liking a particular sport. Would they talk about your stocks and portfolio? I hope not. Wouldn't it be great to be known as a person who prayed and knew the Lord?

## LEAD BY EXAMPLE

When it comes to prayer, more is "caught" than "taught." The greatest way you can leave a legacy of prayer is by praying with people. Someone may come up to you and ask you to pray for them about something that is going on in their life. The best thing to do is stop right then and pray with them. If it's a phone call, pray with them over the phone. Maybe it's a text message. You can pray that way, too. Really talk to the Lord with them, make it a significant time. Another thing you can do, after people have asked you to pray for them, is go back to them and ask how things are going. If you have a prayer list as we talked about before, you can write down that request so you will be reminded to go back and talk to them. If you find the prayer has been answered, you can make a note of it on your list. And you can celebrate with that person how God delivered!

Dr. Roscup, my seminary professor, wrote a 1,000-page book on prayer. As I stated earlier, I asked him to pray for a nearly impossible request. I was in seminary with all men. I was in a church of 200, but there weren't too many girls my age. I had just been through college with 8,000 girls my age, but didn't date much and met no one I would consider marrying. My request to this professor was , "Would you pray that God would find the girl I'm supposed to marry?" Well, within a few months I had met the girl God had for me – through a strange series of circumstances - and we were engaged and about to be married. One day this professor came to me and said he had been praying for me and asked how it was going. I had to sheepishly say, "Oh, I'm sorry. I forgot to tell you. About three months ago I met this wonderful girl and we are engaged to be married." He said, "Great. Another answered prayer!" When you go back to people and ask them how it is going, it lets them know you are praying for them and it means a lot.

Another way you can leave a legacy of prayer is by teaching others to pray. There is an old saying that you can either give a man a fish or teach him how to fish. I hope there are people in your life that you are discipling. No matter what level you are in your spiritual life, you can disciple people. If you have just been saved, find another person who has just been saved and the two of you can learn together. Once prayer becomes important to you, you can teach other people to pray.

## PRAY FOR THE "UNKNOWN" PERSON

The last thing I would like to suggest, if you are going to leave a legacy of prayer, is for you to pray for people who don't exist. Well, maybe they do exist, but you don't know who they are. For instance, people have said to me they are praying for their daughter's future husband, or praying for a person who is going to be their leader. Pray for people whose names you don't even know. Remember, you are praying to God, who does know and who delights in giving His children good gifts.

I hope that 40 Days of Prayer has helped you. I trust you have learned some things about prayer and have been getting better results from your prayer life. I would encourage you to write down one or two things that have changed in your prayer life because of 40 Days of Prayer. Prayer in the present is great but prayer passed on is an irreplaceable gift. Leave a legacy of prayer.

CPSIA information can be obtained at www.ICGtesting.com
Printed in the USA
BVOW11s0009060314

346845BV00004B/9/P